For Ellen and Mike

with deep appreciation for all you do
for me and the congregation and with
affectionate prayers for your New Year

Fondly

Bertram W. Korn

76-5737

JEWISH MEDALS

From the Renaissance to the Fall of Napoleon (1503-1815)

Repeal of Edict Expelling Jews
from Prague

JEWISH MEDALS

From the Renaissance to the Fall of Napoleon (1503-1815)

by Daniel M. Friedenberg

Curator of Coins and Medals
The Jewish Museum, New York

Published for the Jewish Museum

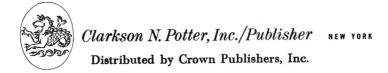

Clarkson N. Potter, Inc./Publisher NEW YORK
Distributed by Crown Publishers, Inc.

For

Acknowledgments

I specially want to thank Dr. Cecil Roth, the well-known writer, who not only gave invaluable suggestions but read the manuscript for errors. Others who have been most helpful are: Mr. Sol Cohen, Hon. Secretary and Curator of the Jewish Museum, Woburn House, London, for opening the files of the English collection; Mr. Henry Grunthal, Curator of European and Modern Coins at the American Numismatic Society, for his cooperation in research and translation of Latin; Dr. Joseph Gutmann, Curator of the Hebrew Union College Museum of Cincinnati, for his making available the medals of the former Kirschstein Collection of Berlin; Mr. Arie Kindler, Director of the Kadman Numismatic Museum of Tel Aviv, for his comments on German anti-Semitic medals; Mr. Julius Margolinsky, Librarian of the Jewish Community in Copenhagen, for his illuminating remarks on Danish material; Miss Olga Raggio, Associate Curator of Western European Arts at The Metropolitan Museum of Art, New York, for making available the card files of that institution; Mr. Siegfried Rosenberg, Registrar of the Jewish Museum of New York, for his patient aid in translating German; Mr. Alfred Rubens of London, for his kind assistance relating to English varieties; and Dr. Menachem Schmelzer, Librarian of the Jewish Theological Seminary of America, for his aid in Hungarian items. Dr. Arthur Polak of Amsterdam and Rabbi Abraham E. Millgram of Jerusalem sent duplicate catalogs of their private collections. Mrs. Bruno Kisch permitted me to check her late husband's collection. The staffs of the various Jewish Museums in Budapest, Jerusalem, and Prague were most cooperative. Madame Marie Chabchay of the Museum of Jewish Art in Paris went out of her way to catalog personally the medal collection. Without such help, the present work would have been impossible.

Contents

Introduction

JEWISH MEDALS, as distinct from biblical medals, exist in relatively small numbers. Aside from the effect of the obvious fact of Jewish tradition, which discouraged the making of graven images, Jewish emancipation in any full sense is little more than a hundred years old. In the strict definition of a commemorative medal—one celebrating an event or a person—there are barely three dozen medals issued in the entire period of history before the fall of Napoleon that deal with specifically Jewish content. The tempo of issuance after 1815 then increased as the nationalist state came into its own and Jews, at last freed from the ghetto, both physically and psychologically, entered into the modern society of Western and Central Europe. By the 1860's, a flood of such medals began to appear. The German Jews were the leading producers. And now Eastern European Jewry, too, started to come out of the imposed cocoon. The first awards to Jews in the United States also appeared in this period. Attempting to catalog Jewish medals after 1860 is a herculean task, for the output has reached tidal-wave proportions. But in the period from 1503, when the first rather mysterious medal of Jewish context was issued, to 1815 or the fall of Napoleon and the beginning of the world as we know it today, the Jewish medal was a rarity indeed.

The author has, therefore, enlarged the scope of this work to include categories that may be considered legitimate. Anti-Semitic medals throw much light on the vicissitudes of Jews in various countries. Medals issued to Marranos and Christian converts tell through their inscriptions—and often through their lack of inscriptions—much about the cultural milieu of the time. And miscellaneous medals, such as those issued to "Jew Brokers" on the London Royal Exchange or as English private token medals, relate a fascinating picture of religious and economic tensions.

1. Anti-Semitic Medals

See Catalog for medals cited

IT IS CLEARLY of interest to observe that, with the exceptions of one Belgian medal and a rather odd English medal, all anti-Semitic medals from early days are of Germanic origin.

The first German anti-Semitic medal was reported in the early sixteenth century.[1] It purported to show on the obverse a Jew riding on a sow and on the reverse the face of a devil with horns. Indeed, such representations were popular in the medieval period. The antipathy of the Jew to swine was converted by a psychological transference (as in the name "Marrano" or "pig" for despised pseudoconverts in Spain) to an identity of Jews with swine. Examples of such German stone satirical decorations can be seen at the city churches of Heilbronn, Magdeburg, Freising, Regensburg, Wittemberg, and Frankfurt am Main. Yet the medal, if it did exist, is not listed in any known museums or collections.

At the end of the seventeenth century appeared the main type of German anti-Semitic medal, called the "Korn Jude," that is, the Corn or Grain Jew. These medals were issued over a period of some eighty years, from 1694 to 1773. They are related to hard times, when prices went up and the popular scapegoat was the Jew, considered a diabolic speculator. Although outside the scope of this work, a variant of the same medal showed up again in 1923, when inflation was rife in Germany.

The prototype of the Korn Jude medal first appeared in 1694.[2] In that year heavy rains and a grasshopper plague swept through Germany in a swath from Silesia to Württemberg. As food prices increased, speculation rose and the starving people blamed the Jews. The Corn or Grain Jew dealer is

1694 Korn Jude
(almost 1½ times)

3

1694 Korn Jude
(*slightly enlarged*)

1694 Korn Jude

shown on the obverse of the medal as a well-fed figure carrying a sack of grain kernels on which a devil is perched, opening the mouth of the sack. "Expensive [or Famine] Time" is the explicit legend below, while overhead we read in large letters, "You Corn Jew." The reverse shows a grain sifter—sometimes described as a ring, a wheel, or a bushel measure—on which is inscribed "He that withholdeth corn, the people shall curse him: But blessing shall be upon the head of him that selleth it." The exergue indicates the origin of the quotation: "Proverbs XI.26."

The 1694 medal was subject to slight variations. Sometimes the Jew faced right, sometimes left. In some cases a landscape appeared behind the Jew, in others not. The grain sifter was either horizontal or upright. The quotation from Proverbs appeared on the outside or inside of the grain sifter or partly inside and partly outside.

A new variety of Korn Jude was struck in 1695. The famine year had passed, and now the medal was stamped "Easy Time." The obverse shows a peasant scene, with a house, barn, and farmland. A Jew is hanging from a tree, with the devil securing the rope around his neck. The inscription, "Luke XII," refers to the chapter of the New Testament which attacks covetousness. On the reverse appear the same grain sifter and quotation from Proverbs.

In the following year, 1696, apparently owing to another bad harvest, the Korn Jude reappeared. There is only one example of this rare medal.

Between 1770 and 1772, after a lapse of more than seventy years, an avalanche of Korn Jude medals was issued. These were terrible years. During this famine period about one hundred and eighty thousand people died of starvation in Bohemia and one hundred and fifty thousand in Saxony. The price of a bushel of corn in Saxony rose to thirteen thalers, the German equivalent of dollars. The reverse inscription of some of these medals is devoted to a list of such food prices, obviously referring to the wild inflation. The typical Korn Jude obverse, showing a Jew with the sack of grain which the devil is opening, is subject to other variations. One curious obverse, dated 1772, depicts a goat, rather than the devil, on the sack. At least, this is the interpretation of L. Pfeiffer.[3] The writer has some doubt, since the figure is shown crouched forward, with extended legs, and if seen on a worn surface it could easily be misinterpreted. But then again, the devil has often appeared in the form of a goat in demonology.

Other obverses from this period are equally provocative. A popular type shows a Jew, sometimes grotesquely fat, walking toward the open jaws of what looks like an alligator. "Fear God" is pointedly stamped on a few. In still others, a woman implores aid of the Jew, who stands with sacks of grain stacked behind him. A rare variant shows the woman imploring while the devil bells the Jew. Another variant, to drive home the moral, has "Go to the devil" inscribed on the rim.

In 1773, whether owing to fine weather or to defeat of the speculators, conditions improved. Now, as in 1695, the theme changes to vengeance. A Korn Jude, apparently struck after the abundant harvest in late 1772, indicates on its obverse a corn harvest and haystack, with the legend "We want this fertility." The reverse shows a Jew hanging in a barn and is labeled "But I did hope for famine time." Another piece, dated 1772 on the obverse and 1773 on the reverse, depicts on the obverse a woman appealing

1695 Korn Jude

Obverse: Jew hanged from tree

Reverse: Similar to 1694

Korn Jude: Linking Dates
1694–1772

1772 Korn Jude: "Fear God"

to the Jew as before; the reverse shows him hanging
from a tree with a legend stating that avarice is the
root of all evil.

Mention should be made of the medalists. This
series is unusual in that the vast majority of all
Korn Jude medals, if not all, were done by only
two men. It is the considered opinion of M. J.
Meissner [4] that the entire group issued from 1694
to 1696 were the work of Christian Wermuth
(1661–1739). Oddly, the initials "C. W." appear
to be engraved on only one piece reported, although
it is apparent these medals are very similar stylisti-
cally. We will return to Wermuth's production
shortly, for he bears the unsavory reputation of
being the foremost anti-Semitic medalist in history.
Records indicate these early Korn Jude medals were
issued in Silesia, though a few are claimed to come
from Hamburg. Wermuth, however, spent his long
life at Thuringia, a state in central Germany, having
been born at Altenburg and died at Gotha. One reason
for this apparent discrepancy may be that Wermuth
produced medals to sell at the annual Leipzig Fair.

The later Korn Jude pieces, between 1770 and
1773, seem to have been made exclusively by Johann
Christian Reich, who signed these medals "Io. Ch.
Reich," "Reich," or simply "R." On many he added
"Fürth," that is to say, issued from Fürth (or
possibly nearby Nürnberg) in Bavaria. As is evident from this stamping, Reich (1740–1814), though
born in Thuringia like Wermuth, moved to Bavaria
at eighteen and spent the rest of his life there. Some
of the larger medals in this group indicate the letters
"C. G. R. U." in the place where medalists often
put their initials, but though the writer has checked
everywhere, he has been unable to discover whom
these presumed initials stand for or what they represent.

It is apparent, when viewing the series as a whole
rather than individually, that the Korn Jude medals
tell the story in metal of the Jew in Faustian terms.

The identification of a Jew with Faust had preceded this period. In the 1604 version of Christopher Marlowe's *Doctor Faustus*, for example, a character explains after being tricked: "Doctor Faustian, quotha? Mass, Doctor Lopus was never such a doctor" —the reference being to Roderigo Lópes, the Marrano physician to Queen Elizabeth who was tried for treason and executed in 1594. The case, involving a charge of poison, already linked a Jew with Faust and set the stage in England for the anti-Semitism that Shakespeare exploited in his characterization of Shylock only two years later.

The Jew as Faust with the awful nemesis that overtakes a man who has sold himself to the devil to gratify his desire for things of the world is told in the Korn Jude series. The devil perched on the sack of grain in "Famine Time" has made a bargain with the Jewish speculator and, opening the sack, appears to be taking his share of the loot. The grain sifter shown on the reverse may be a similar symbol, separating not only the physical grain from the chaff but also the souls of the blessed from those of the cursed, as evidenced by the accompanying quotation from Proverbs. The further reference to Luke 12 on some Korn Jude obverses reinforces the curse of God, adding the weight of the New Testament to that of the Old Testament, as was often done in this period. But the Jew is a difficult prey even for the devil, who is belling him on another Korn Jude medal precisely when the Jew is withholding aid from an imploring woman. On still others, often grotesquely fat from his spoil, the Jew is seen walking straight into open jaws, which probably represent gaping hell. "Fear God," but the Jew does not; and "Go to the Devil" he does, as the inscriptions relate.

The Jew is doomed by his bargain, as shown by the 1695 and 1772–73 Korn Jude medals, struck when "Easy Time" returns. The devil, like men do in the fields, reaps his harvest now—the Jewish speculator. This is clearly indicated in the

1772–1773 Korn Jude

Obverse: 1772—Woman
imploring Jew

Reverse: 1773—Jew hanged

first of these medals, dated 1695, by the devil securing the rope around the neck of the Jew. In the second, whose obverse is dated 1772, a Jew dressed as a cavalier, with stacks of corn behind him, ignores the plea of a woman. The legend reads "Poverty is weeping while the Corn Jew is laughing." On the reverse, dated 1773, the Jew hangs from a tree with a tall harvest in the background. The legend triumphantly states "Avarice is the root of all evil." This is the answer to the Jew's "But I did hope for famine time." The cycle is complete, the devil has taken the Jew, and the admonitions of Holy Scripture have been proved.

It is important to remember that the evangelic message of the Korn Jude series was not regarded as mere metaphor. For the persons who carried these medals as talismans, they told incontrovertible truth. The Faust story, the devil, and hell were real. What we consider a poetic allegory of the human condition was living reality to these people. For example, Prynne in his *Histriomastix* (1633) describes "The visible apparation of the Devill on the stage at the Belsavage play-house in Queen Elizabethes dayes (to the great amazement both of the actors and spectators) while they were there prophanely playing the History of Faustus. . . ." In another case, the play was brought to a sudden close when it was realized "there was one devell too many among them." And the panic this created was described in a third apparition of the devil, when the terror-stricken spectators flung themselves from the window and sought hiding places.

The Faustian legend originated in Germany, and Marlowe's play went back to that country in translation. German versions were very popular in the seventeenth and eighteenth centuries. The Faustian figure was deeply a part of the German folk consciousness even before that time, through the media of Faust books and ballads. It was natural, indeed one might almost say it was inevitable, that some

linking of Faust to the Jew would take place. For
this reason alone, the Korn Jude medals reveal
important insights into the social and religious history of Germany in these two centuries. The advent
of a man like Hitler in Germany, as distinct from
other countries, can only be understood within the
context of such a history.

It should be stated that a part of this anti-Semitic
feeling was based on economic fact. Jews (as well as
Christians, particularly peasant hoarders) speculated
in grain harvests, driving up the prices. Also during
this period, the so-called Court Jews were sometimes
mint masters and debased the currency. But ignored
was the equally obvious fact that the Court Jews
either acted on instructions from their masters (as in
the case of the Prussian Jewish mint masters under
Frederick the Great) or were forced into currency
debasement by the onerous demands of their patron
princes (as was Joseph Suskind Oppenheimer, the
famous "Jud Süs," financial minister to the Duke
of Württemberg).[5] Some of the anti-Semitic feeling
was without doubt suppressed hatred for the rapacious
rulers as well, which was diverted to the Jewish
hirelings: a measure of this truth can be seen in the
interesting fact that after the French Revolution and
up to the 1848 German revolution, no anti-Semitic
medals appeared.

Another type of German anti-Semitic medal is
called the "Feder Jude," that is the "Feather Jew."
These medals all appear to have been issued around
1700,[6] though none were dated. There is general
agreement the medalist was Christian Wermuth,[7]
whose initials are engraved on the most common
variety.

There is no accord as to the exact meaning of the
Feather Jew medals. The obverse shows a Jewish
merchant, wearing glasses, with a hat from which
several feathers extend. He is leaning over, usually
to the left but in one variant to the right, peering into
the contents of what seems to be a small sack or

Obverse

Reverse

moneybag. On his back is tied a large sack. The moneybag is inscribed "Vitia Aliena" or "Faults of Others"; the large sack is inscribed "Vitia Propria" or "One's own Faults." A rare variant also has the words "The Trial" on the large sack. Around the obverse in double lines appears a legend in German, "I wear the feathers which everybody can see; another wears them as a decoy." Again, another variant substitutes the word "horns" for "feathers" in this legend. Underneath, in mixed German and Latin, is inscribed, "Hey thou Feather Jew, know thyself."

The most common Feather Jew medal has on its reverse in alternate Old German and Latin a rhyming stanza that is difficult to translate. A loose translation would be: "Do not ridicule a cuckold, for it is very true that many came to public office by their horns." According to Dr. Bruno Kirschner,[8] small variations occur in this stanza, such as "Talk no ridicule of a cuckold" in the first couplet, and "that some bunglers came to public office through their horns" in the second couplet. On the rim is engraved, "It is a fact that everyone should watch carefully his own wife."

It is difficult to interpret this symbolism. Henry Grunthal, Curator of European and Modern Coins at the American Numismatic Society, tends to the view that the medal is a hybrid, that the obverse and reverse sides do not belong together. Dr. Antoine Feill also classifies this as a mongrel medal.[9] Their view is supported by the fact that many Christian Wermuth medals are found in such hybrid combinations. Dr. Arthur Polak[10] avoids explicit interpretations, simply stating that the term "Feather Jew" is used in abuse like the slang "Yid." Dr. Bruno Kirschner[11] draws attention to the erotic symbolism of "feathers." He then points out the importance of the rim inscription, where everyone is warned to pay attention to his wife. It is his opinion that Wermuth cautions people to watch the Jews, who pimp for the rulers and nobility. The Jews procure for money, and the cuckolded husbands are rewarded by public office.

The writer agrees with Dr. Kirschner. He feels
there is a meaning and consistency tying together both
sides of the Feder Jude medal. The feathers in the hat
of the Jew are set back like the horns of a bull or goat.
Because of parallel legends on this and other medals
of Christian Wermuth, the reference to feathers appears to be used in the same sense as horns in cuckolding: it has already been noted that the two words are
employed interchangeably on the obverse legend. The
Jew wears the feathers; he is a spiritual cuckold and
has no pride. But the Jew also elevates other men by
procuring their wives for the rulers and rewards the
cuckolds by public office. The Feder Jude medal must
specifically refer to the power of the Court Jews, then
at their height, and so hated by most Germans.

There appears to be another meaning as well.
The Latin words "Vitia Aliena" on the moneybag im-
plies that a Jew is disturbed by the faults of other
people only when they affect his pocket. The same is
true for "Vitia Propria" (his own faults); they are
nothing to him, which is why he can carry such a
large sack of them—they are "feathers." [12] This kind
of play on words is quite common to the German
satiric tradition and would seem to explain the term
"Feather Jew." Dr. Kirschner carries this idea one
step further, counterpoising "Vitia Aliena" against
"Vitia Propria." He believes that Christian Wermuth
may have been alluding to the opening verses of
Matt. 7, where the mote in one's eye is compared to
that in another's, with the stern admonition to final
judgment. The variant with the words "The Trial" on
the sack would be relevant to this interpretation. The
Jew is a Pharisee, and as he judges, so shall he be
judged.

Another Feder Jude type exists, sharing the same
obverse with the main type except that in some cases
the Feather Jew is shown without the accompanying
legends. The reverse comes in two variants. On one, a
winged cupid holds a bow and arrow in his right
hand, while by means of a bridle held in his left

Feder Jude
Variant

hand he guides a lion looking back to him. On the other, the same winged cupid is astride a more dragon-like lion, while another similar but wingless figure sits facing him. The Latin legend is *Amor Vincit Omnia*. Even Jews can be conquered by love, seems to be the sardonic implication of Wermuth. Dr. Kirschner, relating the figures astride the animal to the Latin legend, describes the cupid as Amor and claims that the kissing cupids refer to the Greek myth of Amor and Psyche.

1687   Pietism Medal

Christian Wermuth also made some miscellaneous anti-Semitic medals, several falling into the category only indirectly. In 1687, while still a young man, he issued a so-called Pietism medal which has some official status, since the rim is stamped "C F P," which, according to Henry Grunthal of the American Numismatic Society, stands for "Cum Friderici Privilegio" or "With Frederick's Permission," this being Wermuth's ruler, Frederick II of Saxony and Thuringia. A Jew appears on the obverse of the medal swathed in a prayer shawl. Overhead the German legend reads, "The Pharisee Risen from Death," while below the medalist stamped, "Matth: XXIII.," referring to verse 23, "Woe unto you, scribes and Pharisees, hypocrites!" The reverse shows a Negro dwarf swallowing a camel while he reaches for gnats that swarm over a pot of flowers standing on a table nearby. The legend, also in German, states "Catcher of Gnats" and "Camel Swallower," referring to verse 24 in the same chapter from Matthew, "Ye blind guides, which strain at a gnat, and swallow a camel." The medal apparently types the Moslem as a Negro and groups the two non-Christian religions together as subjects for missionary zeal.

A nastier medal (or rather, two variant medals on the same theme) was struck by Christian Wermuth around 1700. Titled from the subject matter as the "False Integrity of Jews, Bad Priests and Tricky Lawyers," the main type shows a wolf and a fox in open country, with sheep in the background. Gaedechens [13] describes the scene as "a fox fleeing from the wolf in sheepskin." An amusing dialogue, much like captions over a modern comic strip, appears in Latin above. The wolf asks: "Why do you flee from me, fox? Don't you see who I am?" The fox retorts, "I know you, I flee from you because you are a rascal under the skin." The reverse is devoted to a German inscription, "He who trusts a wolf in the woodland, a Jew by his oath and a bad priest and tricky lawyer by their consciences, will be bitten by all four"— though the verb "bitten" is a kindly substitute for the vulgar word used. On the rim is added, "Look whom you can trust." According to Meissner, the medal was issued to attack a priest by the name of F. J. Mayer.

A rare variant, mentioned only in Moritz Stern,[14] shows a pack of wolves hunting in open country, rather than the wolf and fox. The same inscription is on the reverse but it is stamped in Old German.

According to Dr. Kirschner,[15] the symbol of the wolf is used by Protestants for both false prophets and the Papacy. He refers to Matt. 7:15, "Beware of false prophets, which come to you in sheep's clothing, but inwardly they are ravening wolves," as the model for this medal. Luther used the symbol of the wolf for the Pope and Milton portrays the same idea in his poem *Lycidas:* "The hungry sheep look up, and are not fed. . . . Besides what the grim wolf with privy paw Daily devours apace, and nothing said."

This medal is evidence that Christian Wermuth embraced Roman Catholics as well as Jews in his general hatred. As an aside, it may also be noted that his preference for Old German spelling, already then obsolete, indicated a general disgust even with Protestant Germany of his own time.

In this same period, Wermuth issued another undated medal which, while a direct attack on the Jews, actually served to compliment them. Called "The Useless Baptism of Jews" or "The Mockery

The Useless Baptism of Jews

Medal," the obverse depicts a Jew kneeling on a rocky shore overlooking water, with a millstone around his neck. A parson stands over him with a prayer book and a bowl of holy water, performing baptism. Behind, an assistant with extended hands comes to push the Jew into the water. The ironic legend states "So he will stay forever": only by drowning at that minute will the Jew stay Christian. The reverse has a long inscription which, freely translated, declares: "A Jew seldom becomes a Christian except when he has done something wrong. He does it only for the money, to avoid serious punishment, for if he would steal he would be punished too hard." To drive the point home, Wermuth inscribed on the rim, "When the mouse eats the cat, then a Jew becomes a true Christian." This German folk expression has been traced back to the Cathedral of Freising, inscribed around 1200.

The last medal in this category was issued in 1728. Very small in diameter, the obverse shows a sailing boat with a mast in the form of a cross. The reverse is filled with an inscription commemorating the beginning of a serious effort to convert Jews and Moslems to Christ.

Of all these medals that Christian Wermuth struck, the most famous is the 1711 "Memorial of the Ghetto Fire in Frankfurt am Main." The Jews in this very old and important ghetto, as elsewhere in Europe, were packed together in a tiny area. Conflagrations would periodically sweep the crowded quarters. In 1711 a very serious fire ravaged the Frankfurt ghetto but by some freak did not damage any of the adjoining buildings occupied by Christians or the nearby municipal gunpowder magazine. This was regarded as a miracle by many Christians, and it was also a perfect subject for the malignant talent of Wermuth. His medal must have been very popular, for it was issued in three slight variant forms and still can occasionally be bought.

Slightly larger than 1 inch in diameter, the ob-

verse depicts the flames of the fire destroying a building, behind which is shown the untouched gunpowder
magazine. In the foreground a father and mother
with two children stand with hands stretched up in
lament. In free translation the Latin legend reads
"And indeed a good thing that in such a manner is
proved"—a vicious comment by Wermuth, approving
the fire because the gunpowder storage depot was
untouched while Jewish property burned.

The inscription filling the reverse is also in Latin.
Again freely translated, it states: "Oh marvelous
event, nonetheless worthy of pity, well to be sure
auspicious, on a happy day that the Frankfort on the
Main Jewish street burned, Rabbi Naphtali the Pole [16]
being the cause. The fire took 24 hours to burn out
completely. Saved from the fire was the Gunpowder
Magazine, saved all the adjoining Christian homes.
The Jewish street started to rebuild on the 23rd of
March when the foundations for the Synagogue were
set, and from there it sprang up. C. W." To emphasize
his feeling, Wermuth added on the rim a quotation
from Plato's *Symposium* which may be roughly ren-
dered, "And I find it right the arbiter of destiny turns
them into ashes," a chilling statement in view of later
history.

It is very difficult to translate the imperfect Latin
of Christian Wermuth (and German experts tell the

1711 Frankfurt Ghetto Fire
Obverse and Reverse
(contact size)

1711 Frankfurt Ghetto Fire
Obverse (enlarged 4 times)

Reverse (enlarged 4 times)

author, likewise his Old German), since the medalist essays all kinds of innuendos and double entendres. But there is also another reason in the case at hand for stilted translation, because both sides of this 1711 medal include chronograms, that is, they tell the date through letters conspicuously different from the others which are then added together by their values as Roman numerals. Of course, the Latin has to be twisted to fit this purpose. The obverse legend is as follows, the underlined letters being of larger size on the medal: AC BONVM QVOD SIC PROBAT. Subtracting the raised letters, we get CVMVDIC, or 100 plus 5 plus 1000 plus 5 plus 500 plus 1 plus 100. The sum of these numbers is 1711, the date of issuance. On the reverse, the second line of the inscription is IVDAEORVM CONFLAGRATA PLATEA. Subtracting the raised letters, we get IVDVMCLL, or 1 plus 5 plus 500 plus 5 plus 1000 plus 100 plus 50 plus 50. The sum of these numbers is likewise 1711, the same date.

The 1711 fire also produced another commemorative medal of great rarity. The obverse has a view of the city of Frankfurt with the emblematic eagle overhead, while the reverse is devoted to an inscription in German, cast in verse form, stating the facts of the fire. The medalist was not Wermuth, but Johann Linck from Heidelberg.[17]

This fire was followed by three others within the decade, and in 1721 Christian Wermuth struck another medal in memory of these fires. The obverse in-

1711 Frankfurt Fire, by Johann Linck

1721 Frankfurt Fires

dicates a view of Frankfurt with burning houses and the eagle overhead. A Latin inscription refers to the four fires within the decade. The reverse inscription, cast in German verse, is most curious. Wermuth mixes Hebrew words in their German form—such as "malachesch" for angel, "zeuhren" for sorrows, and "tschuba" for repentance—to curse the Jews and warn them they will be destroyed unless they convert. The date is again established by a chronogram on the obverse.

1686   The Jews and Turks
Defend Budapest

The only Austrian anti-Semitic medal is early in origin, dating from 1686. It also is satirical and relates to the conquest by the Hapsburg armies of Budapest, the city of Buda, in those days being called Ofen. The Jews, so badgered in Europe, had found their lot much easier under the tolerant Turks. But by the seventeenth century the Austrian emperors, most of whom were anti-Semitic, began to push the decadent Turks out of Central Europe. Budapest fell to Leopold I in 1686. The Jews had sided with the Turks in the defense against Christian attack, and a medal was issued accusing the Jews, with the Turks, of making money out of the war. The obverse shows a Turk and a Jew melting metal in a furnace, the Turk holding the tongs and the Jew the bellows, while ingots appear at the furnace bottom. The German legend states: "Who mints money for peace now that the Turk and Jew are tired of war?" On the reverse of this extremely rare medal the inscription reads: "Ofen belongs to Leopold. Luck has been against Mohammed. He loses the city of Ofen with all its gold, which was destined to be used for the purchase of peace"—a reference to the time-honored method of buying off the opposing army when luck was going against the defenders. The rim triumphantly adds: "By this battle the Turkish Empire nears its end." It may be added that after the conquest, the Jews were driven out of the city and were not permitted to return for almost a century.

It is apparent from some of these anti-Semitic

medals that certain Germans in this period had a fixation about Jewish sexual power, comparable to the fear certain Americans show toward reputed Negro virility. This thread runs through the Feder Jude medals. Without doubt it is related to the Korn Jude medal, where it appears that a goat is substituted for the devil. But the climax in this matter was reached in the case of "Jew Suess," Joseph Suskind Oppenheimer, who was imprisoned and then hanged in 1738 after the death of his patron, Duke Karl Alexander of Württemberg. The joy was so great that several medals were struck to memorialize the event. Almost alone, they tell a part of the social history of eighteenth-century Germany. "Jud Süs" was noted as a gallant, and the most common medal portrays him bewigged as a typical aristocratic cavalier. The reverse shows the gallows scene, with Suess hung in a bird cage (his remains actually hung in the air six full years), and carries the triumphant legend: "Look, in this bird cage you may see/A villain; Suess the Jew, is he."

There are several interesting variants. In one, the reverse of the medal is divided into two parts, an upper and a lower. The top part shows Suess trying to escape in a carriage, calling "Away, Away." Beneath we see a cart being pulled toward the gallows, from which a man is dangling, with the admonition: "This is where you belong." The medal is based on actual fact, for Suess was allowed to escape by a Jesuit faction fearing incrimination, but the Protestant Stuttgart Civil Guard caught him before he got out of Württemberg.[18]

In another, which is quite philosophic in mood, the obverse shows Suess with a halter around his neck and a beard; oddly, the face is thinner and more handsome, and the representation is definitely not a caricature. On the reverse, four persons stand at the foot of the gallows and seem to stare meditatively. The legend states: "As a Finance Minister I felt high and proud. Now as a reward I must hang in the cage."

The most curious variant shows a spray of flow-

Standard Jud Süs Medal
(*approximately 1½ times*)

Jud Süs Trying to Escape

Jud Süs with Halter
Around Neck
(*approximately 2 times*)

ers to the left of the bust, while on the reverse a pigeon flies toward the victim with a billet-doux in its mouth—an allusion to the fact that some woman still cared. Obviously, the figure of Suess reinforced all the myths of Jewish sexual power felt by the German peasantry. In fact, Jew Suess made such an impression that little pictures—some hand painted on parchment and others on tiny copper plates—were drawn to illustrate episodes of his life and fitted into a case the size of the original medal, the obverse and reverse of the box being engraved exactly to match the bust and gallows (or the attempted escape) scene on the medal. The writer has seen one such set, with nineteen pictures, the emphasis being on Suess's romantic life and his trial and hanging. This type of miniature work was a German specialty, and the boxes were called screw medals because the two sides screwed together. According to Dr. Bruno Kirschner,[19] the image of Jew Suess was so strong, these screw medals continued to be made up to the nineteenth century.

As mentioned before, in the period being discussed there were only two anti-Semitic medals issued outside German-speaking territory, one in Belgium and the other in England.

The Belgian medal (or medals, since there were two struck for the same occasion) dates back to 1670, but it memorializes a still earlier event. In 1370 several Jews at Enghien were accused of desecrating the Host, the consecrated wafer used in celebrating Catholic Mass. After a trumped-up trial, their wealth was confiscated by the Church, and they were burned alive at Brussels. The reactionary elements in Belgium made this event a kind of national holiday and struck 300th anniversary medals, showing the Holy Sacrament on one side, with one medal having the seal of the community and the other an inscription on the reverse.

Though outside the time scope set for this work, these bitterly anti-Semitic medals are unique in that the tale has a happy ending. In 1820, 450th anni-

Screw Medal of Jud Süs
(17 of 19 shown, slightly reduced)

versary medals were again issued, replicas of the
1670 medals. This was during the reaction following
Napoleon's defeat and, as before, the claim was made
for national unity, one reverse being again inscribed
as "Jubilee and Communal Holiday of Brussels."

But it was no longer the same Belgium, for the
seeds of new attitudes had already been sown. The
year 1870 was the 500th anniversary. The very popular mayor of Brussels in this period, Jules Anspach,
was a Jew. Liberal and Socialist sentiment was rife.
Indeed, even the Church was divided, and Pope
Pius IX opposed celebrating the event. The medal was
issued but, rather than anti-Semitic, it was philo-Se-
mitic. The obverse shows two Jews being burned (one
in face and stance looking like Jesus on the Cross),
with fat priests taking money from a chest, one holding the coinbags with a gloating expression. The
ironic legend on this side is "Saint Sacrament of
Miracles at Brussels 1370," the plural indicating the
monetary basis of such miracles. The reverse side is
filled with an inscription:

> In 1370 Jews were taken and burned alive at
> Brussels under the pretext of having profaned
> the Host; their property was confiscated and all
> their coreligionists proscribed.
>
> It is the 500th year of a cruel act of spoliation
> and intolerance that the priests wished to cele-
> brate in great pomp this year. Popular sentiment
> has repulsed it with energetic indignation.

The unique English medal in this category, issued in late 1809 (a fact known by the attendant circumstances, for the medal is not dated) has an unusual
background.

The obverse shows a male bust, with long ears
like horns, a full, aquiline nose, sensual lips, and an
extended beard; though intended as a caricature, the
effect is very masculine. Around the outer rim runs
the rhyme, "Yet blush we must for 'tis a nations
shame/Av'rice and titled lust, alone we blame."

Around the inner rim is another rhyme, "This is the Jew, which Shakespeare drew." Beneath is inscribed "No Private Boxes." The initials of the engraver are "V. P."

The reverse has another rhyme in small letters on the rim: "The dramas laws, the dramas patrons give. And he who lives to please, should please to live." Within two sprigs of oak leaves with acorns, tied together by a trumpet and a rattle, are the words, "What d'ye want?"; these are followed by "OP OB & DPO."

It has long been known that "OP" stood for Old Prices, and referred to the Old Price Riots of 1809. Covent Garden, burned down the previous year, had been rebuilt on a grander scale, and a new scale of prices had been introduced. The British public had rioted because of the higher prices. But no other meaning could be found for this particular medal.

The key was located in a long satirical poem by Thomas Tegg, published in London in 1810 and entitled *The Rise, Progress and Termination of the O.P. War.* The details of the medal are actually enumerated in a footnote of Tegg's book on page 111. "V. P.," the supposed engraver, stands for "Vox Populi." "OP OB & DPO" stand for "Old Prices—Open Boxes—and Deference to Public Opinion." What develops is a fascinating piece of English history.

When Covent Garden reopened with much higher prices on September 18, 1809, pandemonium broke loose. John Philip Kemble, a noted actor and also manager of the theatre, tried unsuccessfully to quell the disturbance. It was known that he and his family, who also were numbered among the actors, received large salaries, and the Kembles were denounced by the audience. The racket continued night after night. Covent Garden was owned by a group of entrepreneurs, most of them aristocrats, and the riots began to take on the form of a popular insurrection.

It was then that the manager conceived of a

"This is the Jew, which Shakespeare drew"

stratagem. Kemble was a friend of Daniel Mendoza,
the great Jewish champion pugilist of England, and
of "Dutch Sam," also Jewish, who succeeded Mendoza as champion. The Jews in general were known as
great boxers (see pages 59 to 61). Through Mendoza
and Dutch Sam, Kemble gave free admissions to some
three hundred Jews handy with their fists and in-
vited them to fill the pit, siding with management in
the dispute.

The contest took an anti-Semitic turn. As Thomas
Tegg wrote, "The Christians on the Public's side,
Mendoza's scholars now defy'd. . . . The victory
was still John Bull's, Who broke some ribs and
crack'd some skulls. . . . The Israelites were sorely
griev'd, They such a beating had received." Placards
paraded in the theatre included such mottoes as:
"John Bull the fighting Hebrews smote"; "Be Britons
still, both true and brave, And ne'er to Jew or
Kemble slave"; and "Oppose, boys, Shylock and his
crew, We'll have fair play—fair prices too."

The medal was issued as part of this war, "Hung
from a ribbon round the neck, And many a waist-
coat serv'd to deck," as described in the rather turgid
poetry of Tegg. The medal's obverse was a double-
pronged attack. Kemble had adapted *The Merchant
of Venice* for the stage in 1795 and, as the outstanding actor of his day, portrayed Shylock many
times. The bust represents Kemble in the role of
Shylock as an actor and as a "Jew"; that is, Kemble
with his Jewish allies is now seen as an actual Jew
in the pejorative sense: "This is the Jew, which
Shakespeare drew." But the other rhyme, attacking
"Av'rice and titled lust," also refers to the moneyed
aristocrats who owned Covent Garden and who were
recognized as being behind the actions of Kemble.

The slogan on the medal's reverse that concludes
with, "And he who lives to please, should please
to live," is a reference to the high salaries of the
Kembles, which was a factor in pushing up prices.
And "Old Prices—Open Boxes" and "No Private

Boxes" states what the public wanted. The most subtle touch is the signing of the engraver as "V. P." or "Vox Populi"; that is, the entire British population was speaking as one voice when issuing the medal.

Actually, the anti-Semitic character of this medal was an isolated feature of English opinion at the time, caused by the unpopular position taken by the Jews under the influence of their pugilistic idols. For the general British climate was far from anti-Semitic. Richard Cumberland's *The Jew,* played in this period, took a Jew as its hero. Maria Edgworth's *Harrington,* performed shortly thereafter, showed the Jew as a gentleman for the first time. Both plays were well received. And Edmund Kean's triumphant appearance as Shylock in 1814, only five years later and a landmark in the history of the theatre, was definitely sympathetic in its interpretation. It is thus obvious that the medal, though protesting higher prices, can hardly be interpreted as reflecting a general odium of the Jews.

2. Marranos and Christian Converts

See Catalog for medals cited

Antonio Gonzalo de Toledo

MEDALS ISSUED for Marranos and Christian converts are very few. Marranos were not anxious to draw attention to themselves and thus were only medalized in a neutral or Christian context. In 1518,[20] for example, a medal was issued for an Antonio Gonzalo de Toledo. We know nothing of the gentleman other than that he was a physician practicing in Lyons, France, and published a work there in 1512. Considering the name of González (common to Marranos), the profession and the fact that "New Christian" refugees poured into France from Spain in this period, the likelihood is that Antonio González was a Marrano.

Three other medals feature Marranos from the sixteenth century. They circle around the names Lópes and Pérez, with a collateral relation to the name Núñez.

Between the fifteenth and seventeenth centuries these were very proud Marrano appellations. Refugees bearing such names poured into the Low Countries and England, as well as into Spanish and Portuguese possessions in the Americas, then fanning to the West Indian islands controlled by Protestant countries. A few examples will suffice. Dr. Roderigo Lópes, mentioned earlier as part of the Faustian legend, was physician to Queen Elizabeth. The first group of Marranos in sixteenth-century England held services in the house of Alves Lópes, about 1540. When the Marrano community re-formed in England a century later, a prominent member was Andreas Lópes—in fact, this English line continued until quite recently, by which time conversions lost it to Judaism. In Newport, Rhode Island, Aaron Lópes was one of the wealthiest merchants before the American Revolution, owning some thirty vessels. In Spain itself, the Lópes family maintained its Marrano heritage long after the Expulsion. A friar by the name of Martín de Santo Spirito, alias Lópes, was uncovered as chief agent in a scheme to smuggle New Christians out of the country.

The Pérez family had a similar background. In Antwerp, the Marrano Lópes and Pérez families intermarried. Manuel Bautista Pérez, the wealthiest merchant of Lima, was burned alive at the stake in 1639—the Marranos of Peru met at his house to pray. One of the unresolved mysteries is whether the well-known Gonzalo Pérez, and his still more famous son, the traitor Antonio Pérez, were of Marrano origin. Jan Albert Goris [21] makes the definite statement that these men were relatives of the Antwerp Marrano Pérez family. Gregorio Marañon, in his biography of Antonio Pérez, contents himself with the remark that they were suspected of having Jewish ancestry. Although a medal was issued for Gonzalo Pérez around 1567 as a death commemorative for his service as secretary of state for Charles V and Philip II (Armand III, 283, L, Anon.)—which reverse has the curious representation of the Minotaur in the middle of the Labyrinth—the writer has excluded the medal from this list because of insufficient evidence.

The Núñez family, tied by marriages to the Lópes and Pérez families, was equally prominent. Hector Núñez was an important merchant in Elizabethan England. A Henriques Núñez lived in Bristol in the middle sixteenth century. María Núñez was a founder of the Amsterdam Marrano community. Joseph Núñez de Fonseca was among the first settlers in Curaçao.

The nexus of these families is clearly seen through the three portrait medals of Antwerp Marranos known from the time. Antwerp, as the depot of the spice trade, was an extremely important commercial center. It was a part of the Spanish empire,

yet outside the constant surveillance of the Inquisition, and many prominent Marranos settled there.
Diego Mendes, whose sister-in-law was the magnifi-
cent Gracia Mendes, had made himself master of the
pepper monopoly. Other rich Marrano merchants
were Luis Pérez and Martín Lópes de Villanova.
Branches of these commercial houses were established
internationally, in England, where Martín Lópes and
his brother Francisco also operated, at Bordeaux
and Toulouse (southern France was also a nesting
place for emigré Marranos), where Antonia Lópes
married and became the mother of Michel de
Montaigne, in Spain and Portugal themselves and
even in the New World. The Marrano families intermarried to guard their fortunes. Marcus Pérez, son
of Luis Pérez, espoused Ursula Lópes, daughter of
Martín Lópes. Another brother-in-law was Marcus
Núñez.

There is no evidence that any of these Antwerp
Marrano families Judaized. What remained with
them was hatred of the Catholic Church rather than
a desire to be martyred for the religion their fathers
or grandfathers had left. When the first waves of the
Reformation struck the Low Countries, the Marrano
mentality was therefore very hospitable. Marcus
Pérez became a leader of the anti-Catholic movement.
Very rich from inheritance of his father's spice trade,
he put his fortune at the service of the Calvinist
Consistory. By 1566 Marcus Pérez was the head of
the Antwerp Calvinists, and his house had become
a veritable chancellery from which Protestant agents
acted on the international scene. Pérez was the prime
banker in charge of collecting funds for resistance
against the Spanish in the Low Countries and, like
many converts, pursued his ideal with fanaticism.
He brought his young wife, Ursula Lópes, into the
movement, his younger brother Luis Pérez (named
after their father), and his brother-in-law Martín
Lópes (also named after his father) as well. In
1567, the aroused government forced Marcus Pérez

to leave the country, and he settled with his wife
and children in Basel, the Calvinist stronghold. In
1568, Martín Lópes was declared a heretic and also
fled, and all his goods were confiscated. The Duke
of Alba shortly thereafter put down the Calvinists,
many of whom fled to neighboring Holland to join
the uprising against Spain, and Flanders (now
Belgium) was retained for the Catholic faith.

The three Marrano medals of the Lópes and
Pérez families are silent witness to this historic
episode. The first, dated 1555, is a portrait of Ursula
Lópes at the time of her marriage to Marcus Pérez.
Probably her betrothed commissioned the medal, for
he was also noted as a collector of medals. The
eighteen-year-old girl, with her bridal veil, looks to
the left, and it is apparent from the set of the face
she knows what she wants. Regretfully, the other
medal of her done twenty-five years later, in 1580,
is not locatable. Life had not been kind. The Calvinist
movement in Flanders had been smashed, the family
fortune wasted, her husband had died as a rather
young man, and she had been left a widow with
twelve children. That year, at forty-three, she died;

Ursula Lópes

Luis Pérez

and the medal itself was probably a death memorial. One wonders if Ursula Lópes ever thought of the God of her ancestors in those bitter last years.

The last Marrano medal was a portrait piece done of the brother of Marcus Pérez, Luis Pérez. This man, following his older brother, had likewise been attracted by Calvinism and was a preacher. All the goods of Luis Pérez had been forfeited when he was declared a heretic. The medal was issued for his sixty-sixth birthday, in 1597, and shows a rather kind expression. Indicating the zeal of a convert, the reverse inscription states in Latin, "In Christ is Life." One must conclude that these upper-class Marranos were already so far removed from the religion of their ancestors that nothing remained but a vestigial, and probably distasteful, memory.

The situation was quite different in Central Europe. Jewish converts in this area were not only hated by their former coreligionists but usually disliked as well by born Christians. Reference has already been made to Wermuth's "The Useless Baptism of Jews."[22] In the case of an unlocatable medal, that issued to celebrate the conversion of Jew Michael of Prague to Protestantism at Nürnberg, Michael must have been a trial for all concerned. The obverse of the medal triumphantly displays the three coats-of-arms of Nürnberg overhead, while below we see the baptism of Jesus in the Jordan. The inscription on the reverse relates how on December 21, 1659, Michael of Prague, originally from Posen, Poland, was baptized into the Christian religion with three distinguished Nürnberg patricians as godfathers. The new name of Michael was Burckhardt[23] Christoph Leonhard, each part of the name being taken from one of the godfathers. But the Protestant triumph was short-lived. One year later the erstwhile Michael converted to Catholicism, and he returned to Judaism as a repentant at the end of his life.

Probably because of such case histories, only later, in the more tolerant environment of the eighteenth century, did German Jews succeed in converting without being held up to obloquy by many members of the Gentile community. A unique medal, dated 1714 and in the possession of the County Museum of Heidelberg, is in fact a godfather penny, presented at the baptism of a Jew by the name of Crainfeld.[24] Toward the late eighteenth century, Cen-

Baptism of Jew Michael

Baptism of Crainfeld
(*approximately 1⅓ times*)

tral European converts were so accepted all stigma
had passed. Two such men are represented, the
Austrian financier Franz Anton von Sonnenfels and
the German painter Anton Raphael Mengs; [25] both
men were baptized so young that neither Jews nor
Gentiles regarded them as anything but old-time
Christians. Yet a residue of tension remained even
under the best of conditions. Dr. Arthur Polak, the
Dutch numismatist, has in his private collection a
memorial medal issued on the death, in 1752, of a
convert to Christianity by the name of Hoedemaker.
The inscription on the reverse states that he was
"an Israelite in whom there was no guile"—a compliment sincerely paid but reflecting much of the
mental framework of the time.

Memorial to Hoedemaker

3. The Slow Rise of Jewish Emancipation

See Catalog for medals cited

THE SLOW RISE of Jewish emancipation is portrayed by revealing medals, which often tell only the surface of the story. The major Jewish medals commemorating stages in this process were issued from the middle eighteenth to the middle nineteenth centuries, a span of little more than one hundred years. We shall be concerned with the earliest group. As far as we know, only one—indeed, the last in date of this group—was struck by a Jewish medalist.

The first of these medals celebrates the repeal of the edict expelling the Jews from Prague and Bohemia. From both a historic and an aesthetic point of view the medal is important. The Jews of Bohemia, and especially of Prague, the capital, were an indispensable link between Western and Central Europe. Deeply rooted after some one thousand years of settlement, they sat athwart the main trading routes: indeed, the fortunes of such Jews as Jacob Bassevi, Samuel Oppenheimer, and Samson Wertheimer (names of such magnitude they enter the general economic history of mankind) partly sprang from contracts to purvey gold and silver to the Austrian state mints from or through Bohemia. In contrast with Germany, it was the Bohemian nobility which engaged in finance, and since they lacked capital, they were dependent for credit either on the Prague Jews or on their foreign connections. It was therefore to the interest of both the aristocracy and the sovereign that Bohemian Jewry be left undisturbed.[26]

On the other hand, the gradual decline of guild craft production in the sixteenth century led to increasing misery on the part of the skilled Bohemian workmen. The anti-Semitism this created was

heightened by the special advantage Jews had in the
export of Czech silver through their international
contacts. This dangerous situation was held in check
only by the protection of the aristocracy. In 1507
and again in 1524 the burghers almost succeeded
in expelling the Jews. In 1541 mob violence grew
so severe that Ferdinand I reluctantly agreed to their
expulsion. But as soon as the excitement had sub-
sided, the king (induced also by a monetary consideration) granted safe conducts and royal permits
to various Jews. By 1549 the expulsion decree had
been nullified, and the Jews had flowed back in again.
The growth of the Czech Estates, in opposition to
the autocratic power of the monarchy, led to a new
danger. Again in 1602 the Diet attacked the Jewish
presence. The success of the burghers would have
sealed the fate of Prague Jewry, who thus greeted
with joy the victory of Ferdinand II over the rising
of the Estates. The total dependence on the Haps-
burgs, however, created a very difficult situation. For
the coming to power of any anti-Semitic ruler could
lead to a new expulsion.

This was precisely what happened when Maria
Theresa acceded to the Austrian throne. War marked
her early years, and in 1741 the French occupied
Bohemia, succeeded in 1744 by the Prussians.
Rumors were circulated that the Jews had leagued
themselves with the invaders. When the Prussians
evacuated Prague in late November 1744, the mobs
sacked the ghetto. The municipal authorities, fearing
an inquiry into their passivity during the looting,
then officially accused the Jews of foreign collaboration. Without hearing both sides of the story—and
an official denial was eventually issued by the
Prussians—Maria Theresa decided on the immediate
expulsion of all Jews from Prague and from the rest
of Bohemia. The edict was announced on December
18, 1744; it was to take effect on January 31, 1745.

All native appeals having been disregarded, the
influential Jewish communities outside the country

began to exert pressure on the Empress. Protests
poured in, those most persuasive being from England
and the Netherlands. The weight of this pressure,
plus strong appeals from the Bohemian noblemen
caught up in the economic squeeze, made Maria
Theresa reconsider. On May 15, 1745, the Empress
revoked the edict.[27]

A handsome medal, almost 2 inches in diameter,
was struck by the Dutch Jews to celebrate the welcome
turn of events. On the obverse the Empress sits on
her throne, scepter in hand, with figures probably
representing Love and Justice on either side. A war-
rior pleads the cause of a rabbi dressed in the costume
of high priest, who stands behind with an arm lifted
in protest. All legends are in Latin. Overhead we
read "Exile Threatened," with the date December 18
beneath. At bottom appears a variation of the quotation from 1 Sam. 22:15 (with the word "king"
changed to "Queen"): "May the Queen not suspect
her loyal subjects of such things in such a way,"
referring to the false accusation that the Jews had
betrayed Prague to the Prussians. A chronogram

Repeal of Edict Expelling
Jews from Prague

formed from the letters of the quotation substantiates this by adding up to the Christian date of 1744.

The reverse has been interpreted as showing the Temple of Jerusalem with a thanksgiving offering being burned in front of kneeling priests. The two twisted columns reputedly from the Temple are indeed in prominent evidence. Coats of arms from England, Holland, Sweden, and Poland adorn the facades, apparently in honor of the countries protesting the edict. The legends are likewise in Latin. Overhead is stated "Decree Revoked," with the coat of arms of Hungary-Bohemia, and directly below, the date, May 15. In the exergue appears a rephrasing of the quotation from Esther 9:28 and referring to Purim: "These are the days that should be remembered by all generations in every country throughout the world." A chronogram formed from the letters of the quotation adds up to the number 3761 which, when added to the 1744 of the chronogram on the obverse side, totals 5505. This is the Jewish year for 1745, when the edict was revoked.

Rather than remembering, the reactionary Austrian court soon forgot its fit of liberality. However, Maria Theresa's son, Emperor Joseph II, was an enlightened despot and resolved to tolerate religious minorities, both Protestant and Jewish. He granted religious liberty to Protestants in 1781 and extended some additional guarantees to Jews as well, though the latter were not granted full civil rights.

Two medals, the latter in four variants, were struck in celebration of this event. The first, issued in 1781, has the bust of the Emperor on the obverse and is inscribed in Latin, "Love and Delight of the Human Race." The reverse shows a memorial with a figure pointing out the words in Latin: "Religious Liberty from Joseph II in his Lands to Protestants and Jews 1781." Around on top it is stated in large Latin letters, "Who Commands that All Live Fully." The medalist was Johann Leonhard Oexlein.

The second, dated 1782, was issued by the Dutch

1781   Edict of Toleration

after the Emperor visited the Netherlands. All varieties show the same bust on the obverses as the 1781
medal with, however, three varying legends. One die
has in Latin: "Joseph II, Holy Roman Emperor,
Ever August. Imperial Tolerance." The second die—
and the Emperor's bust is slightly larger as well
—reads the same, but "Imperial Tolerance" is on a
scroll. The third die, with the largest bust of all,
excludes the words "Imperial Tolerance." The
reverses of the above varieties show three figures
under the Imperial Eagle, each representing a religious faith—Catholic, Protestant, and Jewish—in the
Austrian Empire. The accompanying Latin legends
state, "Under his Wings All are Protected" and
"Behold. Friends. 1782." The fourth, and the rarest
variant, has the same bust on the obverse but shows
a kneeling figure next to an altar on the reverse.
Above the figure is "Amicissima Veritas," and in
small letters on the side of the altar is "Lib. Ergo."
Ironically, the medalist for the 1782 medals is
Johann Christian Reich, famous for his anti-Semitic
Korn Jude medals struck shortly before this decade.
It may be added that immediately after the death of
Joseph II, the former restrictions were reimposed by
the Austrians.

The other major emancipation medals from the
eighteenth century were struck by the Jews of Hesse
and Darmstadt, a German princely state. Landgrave
Ludwig X, later Great Duke Ludwig I by grace of
Napoleon in 1806, was of tolerant nature. His wife,
Landgravine Louise Caroline Henriette, was a pro-
nounced liberal and an unusually gifted lady as well.

The first medal, issued around 1777, may have
been unique. The subject was the birth of a son to the
rulers, later the Great Duke Ludwig II. We know
nothing more, for there are no photographs and the
date is established only by the time of the birth of
the child. Issued in gold, the medal formed part of
the collection of Otto Goldschmidt of Gotha; when the
collection was retrieved after World War II by the

1782 Edict of Toleration

Variants of Obverse

Reverse

1790   Medal for Landgrave
Ludwig X of Hesse-Darmstadt

1790   Medal for Ludwig X's
Wife
(*slightly reduced*)

father of the writer and was presented to the Jewish Museum of New York, this was one of a half-dozen medals that had vanished.

The other medals issued by the Jews of Hesse and Darmstadt are both dated 1790, when Landgrave Ludwig X acceded to the throne. They were separate commemoratives to the royal couple. That dedicated to Ludwig shows on the obverse a woman sacrificing at a narrow table. The legend above states in a free translation of the Latin from Horace "Someday Heaven will Reward Him"; beneath, another Latin phrase reads "From the Hessian Jews a public votive offering." The reverse contains an abbreviated inscription in Latin, "Ludwig X. Landgrave of Hesse. Best Prince. Father of His Country."

The medal dedicated to Ludwig's wife, who in fact was the party inspiring religious freedom, shows on the obverse a palm tree, representing ancient Judaea. A finely printed legend overhead states in German rhyme, "Flourish always with new power. This is the wish of the Jewish community." The reverse is an inscription starting with the Latin word "Vivat" or "Live!" and is followed in German by "Louise Caroline Henriette Landgraefin of Hess-Darmstadt. 1790." A very slight variant occurs in that the original die broke after several strikings and

*Variant of Obverse of
medal to left
(approximately 2 times)*

a second one was made, the latter lacking a period following the legend on the obverse. Another, smaller medal was also issued for the same occasion; the obverse legend is indicated in a double line, and the palm has such long fronds that the medal gives the curious impression of a tree wearing a wig.

The only other eighteenth-century emancipation medal was issued as a consequence of the French Revolution. This event was the first great sustained breakthrough for European Jewish emancipation. Curiously, its sole medallic representation does not come from France, but rather from Holland. Political equality had come to the Dutch Jews in 1796 after the troops of revolutionary France invaded that country and formed the short-lived Batavian Republic. A very rare medal, struck precisely in 1796 and now known only in the Royal Coin Cabinet of The Hague, commemorates the equal rights granted to Jews. The obverse shows leafy twigs grouped around an emblem surmounted by a hat, the crest of the Batavian Republic. The reverse has an appropriate dedicatory inscription in Dutch.

Three other Jewish emancipation medals, all encircling the Napoleonic flame, were issued in the first decade of the nineteenth century. The initial one was struck by Czar Alexander I in the flush of his early idealism, when he freed the Jews in 1805 from a special tax—though not from restricted living areas. The bust of the Czar dominates the obverse with "Alexandro" overhead. The reverse shows an erect man, hands clasped in thanksgiving before an altar, and "Liberatori" above. Below, in the exergue, is stated in Latin, "The Jews freed from burden. Feb. 9, 1805." The initials "P. M." stand for Paul Merker, the medalist; his identity had not been established for many years. It is thought by some writers that the medal was struck outside Russia and that a unique piece in gold was presented to Alexander I. This seems to be substantiated by the fact that this medal precedes by many years any other issuance of the

Equal Rights for Jews
in Holland

Czar Alexander I Frees the
Jews from Special Tax

The Grand Sanhedrin of
Napoleon

Russian Jewish community. Note should also be made that Paul Merker, the medalist, came from Brunswick and this medal therefore might have been commissioned by the Jews of Berlin.

The Sanhedrin medal struck by the French mint in 1806 is perhaps the most famous individual medal dealing with a Jewish event. Indeed, the medal is still so popular it continues to be restruck by La Médaille, a branch of the French government, and can be obtained in either silver or bronze for a small sum.[28]

Napoleon was a realist. He needed Jewish soldiers and could not have them so long as they were compelled to follow religious dietary restrictions.[29] To attain this aim, he called a Sanhedrin (the first in some fifteen hundred years) representing the Jews of France and Italy. A logrolling agreement was then reached. Jews were freed from dietary obligations when fighting in French armies and in turn received religious freedom and state protection in the French empire.[30] The Sanhedrin medal was struck to celebrate this occasion. The obverse is a typical sycophantic Napoleonic medal. The idealized bust faces right, with a legend "Napoleon Emperor and King." Denon, Director of the French Medal Mint, put his name alongside that of DePaulis, the actual engraver. The reverse was done by Dupres, another engraver. The Emperor, crowned by laurel and with a mass of chest decorations over a long robe, stands augustly to the left. Facing him on the right is a very muscular Moses, showing horns on his head, most skimpily dressed and barefooted. Moses has just handed the Tables of the Law to Napoleon and is obsequiously bowing; indeed, he almost seems to be clutching the robe of the Emperor! Below in the exergue we read "Grand Sanhedrin XXX Mai MDCCCVI."

Jerome Bonaparte, proconsul for his brother across the Rhine, enfranchised the Jews of Westphalia two years after the French action. The medal has additional interest in that it was engraved by the great Jewish medalist, Abramson; it is one of the last

he did. The design is classic. The obverse shows a
woman in prayer before an altar against which rest
the Tables of the Law. At her feet lie broken chains.
Above, slightly to the right, the Latin legend reads
"To God and the Fatherly King." The reverse is
dominated by two handsome cherubim, one representing Christianity and the other Judaism, with the Latin
legend overhead, "United in the Kingdom of Westphalia."

It should be noted that the native Germans
promptly revoked this edict when they regained
power. Czar Alexander I also got over his fit of youth-
ful idealism and returned to orthodox reaction. Only
in France did the Napoleonic Code remain, insuring
Jewish political equality. The ante status quo established by the European powers after the fall of Napoleon involved in most cases a return to pre-emanci-
pation Jewish policies as well. It was not until the next
leap forward of liberalism, namely, the series of rev-
olutions of 1848, that ordinary run-of-the-mill Jews
as Jews—as distinguished from converts or rich Jews
who bought exemption—became normal citizens with
established rights.

Enfranchisement of Jews
of Westphalia
(*approximately 2 times*)

4. Medals Commemorating Individual Jews

See Catalog for medals cited

Elia Delatas and His Mother, Rica Delatas

MEDALS COMMEMORATING individual Jews first appear in Renaissance Italy, where the Jews participated in the economic and cultural revival. Three appeared during the 1550's.[31]

The earliest, dated 1552, was issued by a son and mother together, Elia and Rica Delatas. It is similar to the many personal medals then in vogue among the rising bourgeoisie of the Gentile community. The faces shown are rather idealized, the man wearing a stylish beard. Perhaps most interesting is the fact that the name of the man is followed by "EBREO" or "Hebrew": the appellation was added voluntarily and was therefore inscribed in pride. Both the grandfather and the father of Elia Delatas were distinguished gentlemen. The grandfather, Bonet Delattes (or de Lattes) was exiled from Provence in 1498 and settled in Rome, becoming a papal physician. He was also an eminent astronomer, inventing an instrument to calculate the altitude of the sun at any time of the day. The father, Emanuele Delattes, was likewise a noted papal physician.

The Lattes family continued to produce eminent members in Italy. Abraham Lattes is recorded as having delivered the city of Cuneo from the siege of the French in 1691, slipping through the enemy lines with news of encouragement. In 1848 Rabbi Abraham Lattes was a member of the governing Assembly of Venice during the Republican Revolution. And at the turn of this century Dante Lattes, a distinguished writer, employed his pen to champion Zionism.

The second Italian Renaissance medal, issued in 1557, commemorates Abramo Emanuele Norsa. Paolo Norsa, who survived the Nazi terror, in the late 1950's published a history of his banking family in two volumes (*Contributo alla Storia di una Famiglia di Banchieri*) which includes a genealogical tree extending back six hundred years—something which many crowned heads in Europe could not do. The Norsas take their name from Norcia, and have produced important members of the Italian Jewish community for hundreds of years, particularly during the Renaissance. Daniel Norsa (late fifteenth century) was a very prominent banker in Mantua. Emanuele Norsa (early sixteenth century), of Ferrara, was considered among the wealthiest men in Italy. Solomon Jedidah Norsa, also from Ferrara in this same period, did original research on the Hebrew scriptures. As a humorous aside, it may be noted that a part of the Norsa family went to England, and the English actress Hannah Norsa was mistress to Lord Walpole, afterward Earl of Orford. Her sister Maria was mistress to Sir Edward Walpole, and Maria's illegitimate daughter Laura (presumed by Sir Edward) married the Duke of Gloucester, brother of George III. The family apparently had talent in many directions.

The Abramo Norsa (1505–79) who sat for this portrait medal was also a banker from Ferrara and a communal leader as well. We know what this medal looks like only from photographs, for it was stolen from the Parma Museum during World War II. It shows the bust of a bearded gentleman facing right, with a stiff brocaded collar surmounted by a lacelike edge, a man obviously conscious of his dignity. The well-known medalist Pastorino de' Pastorini executed this medal, which is one-sided.

It may be added that the Norsa medal probably has not been destroyed, though it has not been recovered. An amateur collector approached the writer and claimed to own the original, which he had bought while on a visit to Rome. The medal shown was a fake of the wrong size. Another fake shows a Christian representation on the reverse, though the medal

Abramo Norsa

is only one-sided. Apparently the thief cast several imitations and has been peddling them to gullible collectors.

In 1558 appeared one of the truly great Jewish medals of all time, the uniface portrait of Gracia Nasi, also considered to be the work of Pastorino de' Pastorini.[32] The Marrano Nasi family which had adopted the name Mendes, developed at Lisbon one of the greatest banking and commercial houses in Europe. The history of this family seems to come straight from fable. When Francisco Mendes, the head of the firm, died at Lisbon, the family already was under the cloud of Judaizing. His widow, Beatrice da Luna and their daughter Reyna, went first to Antwerp and then to Constantinople, under the Turks. There they openly avowed Judaism, and Beatrice da Luna became known as Gracia Mendes. Extremely liberal with her enormous fortune, the mother was the most respected Jewish woman of the age. Reyna, the daughter, married her cousin João Miguez, now known as Joseph Nasi. It was this Joseph Nasi who became in his subsequent career virtual ruler of the Turkish empire, then the most powerful in Europe. He was created Duke of Naxos and the Cyclades, which he governed through the offices of a new Christian, reputedly a descendant of the Senior family who administered the royal finances for Ferdinand and Isabella of Spain.[33] He attempted to revitalize the industry of Tiberias in Palestine, establishing a Jewish colony for that purpose. He made and unmade wars in Europe, gaining Cyprus for the Turks. He aided the revolt of the Netherlands against Spain as an act of personal revenge for the expulsion of the Marranos. And Joseph Nasi recouped the fortunes of the family wherever they had been confiscated. According to Dr. Cecil Roth (*A History of the Marranos*): "No professing Jew in recent history has ever attained such power" (p. 203).

The medal depicts the bust of a young lady of

Gracia Nasi
(*contact size and enlarged*)

eighteen peering to the left, dressed in the height of
Renaissance style with a rich brooch hanging from
her neck. The costume is similar to Pastorino medals
of Girolama Sacrata, Cicilia Bonzagna, and Catarina
Bonzagna, all done in the same period. We can tell
from the date that this is not the Beatrice da Luna
who became known as Gracia Mendes, but rather her
niece and namesake. Joseph Nasi had a brother, Samuel Nasi, who married this other Gracia. Samuel Nasi
tarried for a while in Ferrara, Italy, where this medal
was cast, probably to celebrate the marriage of the
young couple. Most significant, the name "Gracia
Nasi" is inscribed in Hebrew letters, the first time
this is seen on a personal medal.[34] Because of the
use of the Hebrew letter *tzadi,* the name appears as
"Gratzia Nasi."

Over one hundred years pass before any other
medals appear commemorating individual Jews. The
reason is the backlash affecting the Jews as a result of
the Counter-Reformation. The Jews had been expelled
from Spain, not recognized in France, and now were
forced into ghettos in Italy. The religious conflict in
the German states and Central Europe was even more
harsh on the Jews than on the Christians. Now the
pendulum swung to the northern countries, mainly to
Holland and England, where the Marrano refugees
flung off the cloak of Catholicism and openly reverted
to Judaism. We know of only three seventeenth-century personal-type Jewish medals, and in all three
cases we have to strain definitions to include them.

The first, issued in 1667, was a presentation by
the Dutch States-General to Josef Athias for publishing an exceptionally fine Hebrew Bible. This Bible,
of which some three thousand copies were sold (an
enormous number for the time), was internationally
recognized by both Jews and Christians. The medal
itself, with the gold chain, is lost. It may be added
that the award was based not so much on aesthetic as
on commercial reasons. The canny Dutch welcomed
the Marranos for their money and shrewd mercantile

sense, and Holland had become the center of Hebrew printing from which the books were shipped all over the known world.

The other two medals are English in origin. Both were issued to Elias Lindo, a broker on the Royal Exchange in London. The first, struck in 1673, was pendant and obviously served to identify the broker when attached to his coat. The obverse shows the royal arms and the reverse the arms of the city of London, with a space beneath to incise the name of the broker.

In 1697 the rules of the Royal Exchange were revised and the number of Jews fixed at twelve. Elias Lindo received a new medal at this time. Henceforth these twelve members, each of whom received a medal, were colloquially known as "Jew Brokers." The Lindo family, whose brokerage medals range from the seventeenth through the nineteenth centuries,[35] gave their collection to the Guildhall Museum in London, where they can be seen today. A later Lindo also married a Norsa, and the last "Jew Broker" medal of this family was issued in 1858 to Joseph Norsa Lindo. The registration of brokers was abolished in the 1880's.

The deliberate limiting to twelve Jews indicates how powerful the seventeenth-century Marranos in England had grown, for it was feared they would dominate the Royal Exchange if more were allowed

1697 Elias Lindo
Royal Arms

1697 Elias Lindo
Arms of City of London

1728 Isaac Lindo Jun.
Royal Arms

1728 Isaac Lindo Jun.
Arms of City of London

entry. This did not deter the rise to great wealth of
the English Sephardic Jews; it was rather conversion
and assimilation that caused their decline. This can be
shown by reviewing some of the most notorious cases.[36]

Sir Solomon Medina, knighted in 1700, accom-
panied the Duke of Marlborough on his campaigns
and was supplier to the army. Though the largest con-
tributor to the Sephardic congregation, his descendants
left Judaism. Sampson Gideon (born Abudiente) was
the friend of Walpole and the most active of the
twelve "Jew Brokers" then authorized. By the mid-
eighteenth century he had reached as high as a Jew
could go and chose baptism for his children. His son
became Baron Eardley; the present Lord Auckland [37]
is in the blood line. A niece of Gideon married Pel-
legrin Treves, and through their son, who converted,
created another distinguished line, including at the
end of the last century the Countess of Loudon, the
Dowager Viscountess St. Davids, Lord Grey of Ruthin,
and the Marquess of Bute. The same occurred with
the most notable financial house of Abraham and
Jacob Franco; their descendants changed both name
and religion. Of the fourteen sons and daughters of
Baron d'Aguilar, the records indicate only one
younger son kept the old faith; direct descendants
are General d'Aguilar and Admiral Keith Steward.
Rich members of the Furtado and Bernal families
converted to rise in the world; Ralph Bernal became
a magistrate and member of Parliament, and the
present Duke of St. Albans [37] is his great-grandson.
John King (real name, Jacob Rey), a leading financier, married the Dowager Lady Lanesborough,
sister of the Earl of Belvedere. The marriage called
forth satiric poems, of which the following is an example:

> Here's a Jew like a King from 'Change-Alley,—
> the smouch
> Now rests on his stick, with one hand in his
> pouch;
> While counting his treasure, he finds more delight,

Than we round a table well spread on Twelfth-
Night
Bless Moses, thinks he, what a chance to succeed!
Two Lott'ries must make a man happy indeed,
While that from the City gives Houses and Land
The other may bring twenty Thousand to hand.[38]

Most cutting was the case of the Ricardo children. Abraham Israel Ricardo, a pious Jew and very
prominent member of the Stock Exchange, watched
his many sons go over to Christianity. One of them,
David Ricardo, not only inherited his father's bril-
liant talent for making money (he died rather young,
leaving the colossal fortune of 700,000 pounds) but
became one of the greatest economists in all history.
The daughter of Percy Ricardo, another son, married
the seventh Duke of Richmond; their son became the
eighth Duke; and his daughter in turn married the
Duke of Northumberland. Immediately before this
occurred the apostasy of a family whose twin roots
extended back to the original English migration,
namely Mordecai Rodriguez Lopez, married to Re-
becca Pereira. Menassah Lopez, son of Mordecai, was
created a baronet in 1805. From this line were descended, through a nephew, Lord Ludlow, Lord
Roborough, and Viscount Bledisloe. It is hardly nec-
essary to note the defection of Isaac d'Israeli, father
of Benjamin Disraeli, the extraordinary prime minister of England. Of the early "Jewish peerages" the
Rothschilds (Ashkenazim in origin) alone were still
Jewish.

These examples are only the most sensational.
Studies have indicated that a good part of the entire
English aristocracy is descended from these Sephardic
converts and that if a more far reaching Nürnberg law
were applied, it could involve the destruction of the
present English nobility. As Dr. Cecil Roth stated
in his book, *A History of the Marranos:* "A generation or two of tolerance sometimes achieved what centuries of persecution had failed to do, and finally as-
similated their descendants to the dominant culture
and religion" (p. 312).

It should be noted that the later migrating Ash-kenazic Jews, mixing with the remaining Jewish Marranos, took up in the nineteenth-century London stock market where the anglicized Marranos left off. Proof of this can be seen in a series of business tokens issued by John Ashby, member of the London Stock Exchange from 1814 to 1838. All tokens alike show on the obverse a bull and on the reverse a bear, adorned with human heads. The head of the bull is that of Nathan Mayer Rothschild and that of the bear is Moses Mocatta; these are not anti-Semitic tokens but, on the contrary, a tribute to the financial genius of the English Jews.[39]

The eighteenth century saw the glimmers of a more general emancipation of the Jews, as Jews per se, and not as pseudo-Jews or Marranos returned to Judaism. As mentioned above, Ashkenazic Jews be-gan to migrate to England, creating a more traditional type of Jewish life. The same movement brought them to Holland. In Germany, Court Jews gained extraor-dinary power under certain princes, even though it was a sycophantic relation which could vanish over-night through an arbitrary act or death of the patron. Especially in Prussia, under Frederick Wilhelm I and his son Frederick the Great, Jews rose rapidly to posi-tions of affluence. This prosperity brought an in-creased level of general culture and with it, if not actual physical assimilation, a more profound cul-tural assimilation. Like the Jews in the Italian Renais-sance two hundred years earlier, the English, Dutch, and German Jews wanted to share in the economic and social life surrounding them. One measure of this participation was the personal medal issued to com-memorate a specific event in the life of a person or to celebrate an outstanding personality: a medal issued not only by the individual himself, as in the Renais-sance, but often for him by others.

These medals fall into natural groupings. There were medals issued to celebrate weddings and anni-versaries. There were medals issued to celebrate at-tainment of a professional aim. And there were medals

issued to celebrate a certain moment in the life of a
very esteemed individual. Examples of all three types
exist.

   The wedding or anniversary medal was already
very common in Holland and Germany among the
prosperous burghers. The Jews living in these countries picked up the custom, though in the eighteenth
century it was still considered exotic. Jacob and
Hanna Bassan, a Dutch couple, reached their silver
anniversary in 1714, and a medal was made to com-

Jacob and Hanna Bassan

memorate the event. The scene presented is typically
Dutch, a harbor view on one side (with, however, a
palm tree standing for ancient Judaea) and an inscription framed in curtains on the other. Still pious,
the dates are inscribed according to the Hebrew
calendar, as the third of Sivan 5449–75. Again in
1749, another couple, presumably Dutch by the Marrano sound of the name, celebrated their golden anniversary by issuing a medal. We knew nothing more
of Benjamin and Rachel Henriques other than this
medal—except the fact that they were evidently prosperous because the piece was issued in gold—since
the sole reported copy disappeared during World
War II.

This custom then spread to the area adjoining
Holland. Around 1780 Daniel Abensur and Sara de
Castro issued, or received, a silver medal at the time
of their marriage in Altona, near Hamburg. As the
inscription informs us, the young man and woman
were born within two weeks of each other in 5513
(1753). Again the names inform us they were Marranos. Probably Daniel Abensur was a direct descendant of the famous Daniel Abensur (died 1711) who
was one of the heads of the Portuguese Marrano community at Hamburg and minister resident of the king
of Poland in that city. And in 1804 the marriage of
N. W. and L. Kaulla was commemorated in Stuttgart
by a silver medal showing a mountainous landscape
worthy of the region.[40] This medal, too, was lost in the
Nazi holocaust. It is worthy of note that the two missing medals of which we possess a description both
pointedly include a palm tree on the obverse, the traditional representation of Judaea.

The two professional commemorations from this
period are both Dutch and celebrate entry into the
medical profession. In 1722 Dr. Abraham Gomes de
Sylva (an obvious variant on the proud Marrano name
of da Silva) entered the Amsterdam Medical Society.
In 1809, almost a century later, B. E. Asser celebrated the same event. The two medals, originally in
the Berlin Jewish Museum, disappeared under the

Daniel Abensur—Sara
de Castro

Nazis. All we now possess of their memory is a sparse catalog description.

The most exciting group of early Jewish medals, aside from those of the Italian Renaissance, are concerned with the Haskalah movement, centered in the Prussia of Frederick the Great. Here we encounter for the first time medals of great Jews engraved by great Jewish artists, namely Jacob Abraham and his still more talented son, Abraham Abramson (or Abrahamson).[41]

The position of the Prussian Jews was rather ambiguous.[42] Both Frederick Wilhelm I and his son Frederick the Great were noted anti-Semites. However, unlike the traditional princes of many German states, these men were willing to use the talents of all subjects, including Jews. Frederick Wilhelm I supplied his silver for the state mints by arrangement with Jewish merchants. Jewish court jewelers, factory owners, and bankers were also growing in prosperity. When Frederick the Great came to the throne his aristocratic disdain for Jews was more than counterbalanced by his keen understanding of their abilities. Jews now became deeply entrenched in all phases of Prussian commercial activity, including the operation of the state mints. The final breakthrough occurred in 1755, when the king leased the six state mints to a Jewish firm consisting of Daniel Itzig, a prominent banker, his brother-in-law the money dealer Moses Isaak, and Hertz Moses Gumpertz, a leading tobacco manufacturer. This firm had beaten in bidding a rival syndicate also formed by Jews, consisting of the Fraenkel brothers, former lessees of the Königsberg and Breslau mints, and Veitel-Heine Ephraim, court jeweler to Frederick. The last step was a merger of these interests, and in 1758, when Gumpertz died, the two firms combined and the king leased all six Prussian mints and the two Saxon mints to the new company.

The men behind this firm became known as "Münz-Juden" or "Coin Jews," so powerful were their interests. They formed a tight Prussian Jewish

aristocracy and attempted to aid and encourage the
less fortunate Prussian Jews—incidentally also co-
operating with Frederick's anti-Semitic policy of
limiting Jewish entry into Prussia from other states.

Jacob Abraham (1722–1800) was one of the
fortunate few. His gift was manifested early, and he
became a top medalist of the age. Through his friendship with the Coin Jews, he was hired to engrave the
royal coins. His son, Abraham Abramson (1754–
1811) was even better known and is considered by
some experts to be the finest eighteenth-century medal
engraver, not only working for the Prussian mints but
as official medalist to the court as well.

We are fortunate that both father and son engraved some of their most prominent coreligionists.
The most important of these medals, struck about
1774, is an homage to Moses Mendelssohn, the very
great leader of the Haskalah movement. Both father
and son collaborated on this work, which without
question is among the dozen most important Jewish
medals ever issued. On the obverse we see facing left
the bust of Mendelssohn, with the overly massive
shoulders butting the head, as is typical of hunch-
backs. The long, searching nose, the high forehead,
the deepset eyes, and thin, fixed mouth all reveal the
restless mind of a scholar. The reverse shows a skull
with a delicate butterfly perched on top, indicative of
the immortality of the spirit. The symbolism refers to
the well-known philosophic work by Mendelssohn entitled *Phaedon,* modeled on the dialogue of the same

Moses Mendelssohn

name by Plato. Happily for collectors, the medal was immediately recognized as an extraordinary piece, and many were struck. From certain imperfections seen on some copies, the writer is of the opinion that either later dies were made or the dies were reused after corrosion.

In 1793, the occasion of Daniel Itzig's seventieth birthday, Abraham Abramson (alone this time, not in collaboration with his father) celebrated the event with another classic production. Daniel Itzig was perhaps the most powerful Jew in Prussia, a prominent banker, owner of lead factories and the Berlin oil mill, director of the Prussian mints, patron of the Jewish Free School of Berlin, and head of the Jewish communities of Prussia. He was Abramson's patron and employer at the mint. The portrait presented is naturally idealized, and yet it is to the credit of the medalist he caught a certain stolid side of Itzig. Like Moses Mendelssohn, who openly condemned the activities of the Coin Jews—which had led to much anti-Semitism because of the resultant inflation—it is obvious that Abramson had mixed feelings toward his employer. The bust of Itzig faces right, and he is dressed in what seems a nightcap and bathrobe. The chin is full, the mouth grimly set, and, unlike the medal of Mendelssohn, there is no hint of good humor in the face. On the reverse stands a figure representing Charity, covering a poor unclothed boy with a part of her mantle and handing him fruits. Above we read in Latin, "Well Deserved," and in the exergue, "In Reverence Dedicated by the Oldest Son, 1793." Apparently the medal was commissioned by the family when Daniel Itzig reached the age of seventy, but the allusions obviously relate to his philanthropic activity with the Jewish Free School of Berlin.

In 1794 Abramson did another portrait medal of a member of the Berlin Jewish circle, this time of Dr. Marcus Herz, well known in his time as both a physician and a philosopher. This is the rarest medal of the three.[43] Dr. Herz faces right, bewigged, in dress and face a typical upper-class German; and indeed,

Daniel Itzig

Dr. Marcus Herz

Lippman Meyer in Breslau

in this sense, the medal cannot be distinguished from a dozen similar medals executed on commission of prosperous Germans in the same period. The reverse shows a classical presentation of Pallas, the Greek goddess of wisdom, and the legend in Latin relates "Being Physician and Philosopher Together in One Made Him Strong." It is not one of the best works of Abramson.

Several former studies give credit to Abramson for producing a medal honoring the seventy-third birthday of Lippmann Meyer in Breslau. This is not correct, for the medal was engraved by Anton Friedrich Koenig, not a Jew. Meyer held a position in Breslau similar to that of Itzig in Berlin, being a royal court agent and patron of the Jewish Wilhelm School. The obverse of the medal portrays the bust of Lippmann Meyer to the right, wearing the usual wig and indicating his name overhead. On the reverse, over acorn branches tied together by a ribbon, we read in German, "A Philanthropist with Good Advice and Assistance." Round the rim is another legend, also in German, stating "On the 73rd Birthday, the 29th of April 1803, Presented by B. F." As indicated by the initials, the medal was commissioned by Benoni Friedlaender, son of the famous David Friedlaender who was the intellectual successor to Moses Mendelssohn in German Jewry.

The last of this group of Prussian portrait medals represents Veitel-Heine Ephraim, one of the leading Coin Jews and court jeweler to King Frederick the Great as well. The medal, possibly apocryphal, is referred to in a single place, on page 97 of *Demokritus* by Karl Julius Weber, Vol. VI. It is reported as showing Frederick caressing the cheeks of Ephraim, with the inscription, "This is my son, a favorite to me," referring to the biblical Jacob's preference of Joseph's son Ephraim over the eldest born Manasseh (Gen. 48:19).[44] The writer can state nothing more, for the piece is not included in any known museum or private collection.

It will be noted that these Prussian Jewish aristocrats, like their Christian counterparts, were all related by marriage and commercial interest. One daughter of Daniel Itzig married David Friedlaender. Another married a son of Ephraim. A third married a son of Mendelssohn and was the mother of Felix Mendelssohn-Bartholdy, the great composer. The financial web between these men has already been touched upon. It must be stated that they shared another point in common—they had reached as high as they could go without actual conversion and were hankering to cross that ultimate line. Implied in the writings of Moses Mendelssohn is the theme that the Jews were really just like everyone else, and it was logical for his children to conclude that if this were true, they might just as well indeed be like everyone else and become Christians. David Friedlaender actually petitioned for baptism if it were not required to believe in the divinity of Jesus. The results could have been prophesied, as indeed they were by the orthodox opponents of Mendelssohn. Within two generations, almost all the descendants of the Berlin circle—including the individuals commemorated on these medals—went over to Christianity. Like the Sephardic immigrants to England, the one thing the Jews could not withstand was prosperity. Their sentiment was well recorded in the ironic line of Heinrich Heine a half century later: "Judaism is not a religion; it is a misfortune."

There are several late-eighteenth-century medals of great interest from other countries, one from Italy and the rest from England.

The sole Italian medal from this period—more truly a token—was a personal issuance around 1780 by Mose Benjamin Foà, a court agent to the dukes of Modena and a very prominent bookdealer and bibliophile. As has already been noted, the Counter-Reformation drove the Jews of Italy into ghettos, destroying both their economic and their intellectual life. In this desert there were a few isolated oases, and the duchy of Modena was one of these.

The Foà family, like the Lattes and Norsa fam-

Mose Benjamin Foà

Obverse

ilies, seems to have engendered remarkable members
over a span of hundreds of years. Mose Benjamin
Foà pointedly refers to this on his private token
medal, engraving his name round the printer's mark
of Tobias Foà, formerly the family badge of this,
his sixteenth-century ancestor, who founded and ran
an important printing house at Sabbionetta. Mose
Foà would have likewise been proud of the family
that followed. Pio Foà (1848–1923)—who incidentally was born at Sabbionetta some three hundred
years after Tobias Foà—was a professor at Modena
and Turin, and became the outstanding Italian anat-
omist of his time. A part of the family emigrated to
France in the eighteenth century, where the name was
sometimes spelled Foi or Foy. To this branch belong
the explorer Eduard Foà, Captain Cremieu-Foà,
Commander Leon Franchetti,[45] and the engineer J.
Sciama. And in our own time, a descendant of the
Italian Foàs was among the Israeli paratroopers who
took Old Jerusalem in June 1967.

The English medals all relate to two fascinating
personalities, Lord George Gordon, the aristocratic
convert to Judaism, and Daniel Mendoza, the boxing
champion of England.

Among all converts to Judaism throughout history, Lord George Gordon was possibly the most
exotic. A younger son of the third Duke of Gordon—
his eldest brother inherited the dukedom—George
Gordon (1751–93) started life as a violent anti-
Catholic fanatic and agitator. In 1774 he entered
Parliament and organized the Protestant Association
to oppose acts of leniency toward Roman Catholics.
In 1780 he headed violent mobs which, directed at
Catholic groups, terrorized the city of London. He
was indicted for high treason, but owing to important
connections he was acquitted. In 1787 he converted
to Judaism and, following his violent and intemperate
nature, tried to outdo the most orthodox Jews in his
piety. The following year he was convicted of libeling
the queen of France and was thrown into Newgate

Prison. There he surrounded himself with an ultra-orthodox retinue of Polish Jews and conducted services. Also in attendance was Kitty Levi, "the little Jewess, the pretty companion of Lord George Gordon," as noted on an etching of Ozias Humphry.[46] He died shortly thereafter, a puzzle alike to both his aristocratic family and the native English Jews, who did not quite know how to handle the situation.

There was a token issued for Lord George Gordon in 1780 and then, following his death in 1793 in Newgate Prison, a series with varying reverses. All the obverses, including the 1780 issue, show a bust of Gordon with a long beard and slouched hat. The reverses do not seem to make sense until it is realized that the tokens were issued by Thomas Spence, considered the first English Socialist and a friend of Tom Paine. It is then obvious that Spence looked upon Gordon as a revolutionary whose real aim was to destroy vested English power. "Rouse Britannia!" is on one reverse; "We were born free and will never die slaves" is on another; Cain killing Abel and "The Begining of Oppression" is on a third; and the most explicit, "After the Revolution" with men dancing, is on still another. Spence, a great admirer of the French Revolution, specialized in such tokens and was arrested three times on charges of sedition and treason. The Lord George Gordon tokens, therefore, form a valuable addition to the social history of eighteenth-century England.[47]

In another way this is equally true of the tokens, also in the English halfpenny size, issued for Daniel Mendoza. Mendoza (1763–1836) was boxing champion of England from 1792 to 1795; he was the first to emphasize skill over brute force. All obverses show the bust of Mendoza to the left, who indeed looks as tough and pugnacious as one would expect. The reverses vary, referring to local situations. Some rims have engraved "On demand in London, Liverpool or Anglesey"; others, "Spence Dealer in Coins London." There is a separate medal issued in 1791 which shows

1780 Lord George **Gordon**

1793 Lord George **Gordon**
(*example of one type of reverse*)

Daniel Mendoza
(*approximately 2 times*)

Fight of Mendoza and Ward

Mendoza boxing with William Ward, another contender.

The fact that a late-eighteenth-century Jew became boxing champion of England is no accident. In that century the popular image of the Jew had changed greatly. During the late seventeenth and early eighteenth centuries the immigration into England had been Sephardic, rich ex-Marrano merchants with international connections, including entree into some of the best English aristocratic circles. By the middle eighteenth century the type of immigrant changed radically. Poor Jews from Germany and Poland started arriving. Persecutions in North Africa brought in a different Sephardic element from Morocco. These immigrants were poor, less cultured, and more attached to Jewish customs that seemed very alien to the average Englishman. The anti-Semitism toward the Marranos based on envy now became an anti-Semitism toward the newer immigrants based on contempt. The rhubarb-and-orange peddler, the vendor of old clothes and rags, became popular subjects of mockery, as can be seen in the caricatures of Thos. Rowlandson. The poor isolated Jew, wandering the streets of London with his box or sack of secondhand goods and fruits, was an object of derision and attack by gangs of boys and rowdies.

The result was that the Jews learned to box in self-defense. In time, the "scientific" use of their fists spread and earned them respect. The crown in this diadem was Daniel Mendoza, the idol of the London mob, whose heroic powers in the pugilistic art destroyed more anti-Semitism in the English population—other than the brief flurry over the Covent Garden riots referred to before—than a thousand learned treatises on the subject could have done. Following Mendoza came "Dutch Sam" (Samuel Elias), "Bitton the Jew" (Isaac Bitton), Barney Aaron, and Abraham Belasco. It can be said that after these men the image of a Jew as a coward and toady never lifted its head in the English popular mind again. As an example of this change of attitude, a humorous ditty of the time records an imaginary visit of the English ambassador to the Spanish king at Madrid in 1790. One couplet states:

Should you wish for a war we have got a new race
Of such brave fighting fellows, not the Devil dare face
A sample I've brought, only four of our men
Mendoza, Dick Humphries, Joe Ward, and Big Ben.[48]

The last personal medal of the eighteenth century has an earlier origin, going back to 1735 in Holland. It is reserved to the end for the medal forms a link with the next group, those issued to commemorate specific Jewish activities. More pertinent, it is a freak in the technical sense, a medal which should never have been struck according to strict Jewish tradition at that time.

The Dutch Community of Jews, like that of England, was divided into two groups, the Sephardim and the Ashkenazim, who can likewise be separated in social and economic terms: the older and the newer immigrants, the Jews of Western Europe and the Jews of Central Europe, aristocrats and plebeians, rich and poor. Though the distinction was never automatic, it was true for the large part. The Sephardim looked down upon the Ashkenazim and did not even grant them entry into their philanthropic activities and hospital facilities.[49] Social contacts were rare; intermarriage, even rarer. When the first Ashkenazim came to Holland, they were snubbed and soon set up their own synagogue (the difference in ritual between the two groups being far less important than the social chasm).

In 1735 the Ashkenazic community of Amsterdam lacked a rabbi, and the Elders called upon the Chief Rabbi of Brody, in eastern Poland. Rabbi Eleazar ben Samuel Shmelka heeded the call, and a medal was struck to celebrate his arrival. Most astounding, his portrait adorns the medal, for it was against tradition that orthodox Ashkenazic Jews

Rabbi Eleazar ben Samuel
Shmelka
(*contact size and enlarged*)

Obverse

would consent to such a representation; or indeed, that Rabbi Eleazar himself would agree. In fact, the medal was violently attacked by Rabbi Jacob Emden, who wrote a *responsum* that it contravened Jewish law.[50] The medal itself is mediocre, the obverse showing the rabbi with an Eastern European high round hat and a beard, the badly sculptured right hand set on an open book. The legend above states in Hebrew "Our teacher, the Rabbi Elazar, son of our teacher the Rabbi Shmuel, President of the Rabbinical Seminary of the Holy Congregation in Brod." The reverse has a very lengthy Hebrew inscription jammed together. The first line states "Received here on Wednesday 27 Elul 495 [5495 = 1735]." Following is a quotation from *Sayings of the Fathers*, Avot 3:2, "Pray for the good of the government." Bisected by a line in the middle of the center of the reverse, in order to make available doubled space, and engraved in small letters, is a series of ten different pious quotations from

Reverse
(*contact size and enlarged*)

Psalm 119. Beneath is still another quotation, this time from 1 Kings 17:22, "And the Lord hearkened unto the voice of Elijah . . . and he revived." The very last line seems to continue the first line, adding "Here Amsterdam." As though this aesthetic mishmash were not enough, the medalist put directly above the last line a group of Hebrew contractions which, in effect, form his personal signature. These state "By the hand of Joel, the son of the honorable Lippman Levi, may he be protected by his rock and redeemer."

This is the first medal known in all history unequivocally to be done by a Jewish medalist.[51]

5. Medals Commemorating Jewish Activities

See Catalog for medals cited

MEDALS ISSUED to commemorate Jewish activities are rare in early days. The Jewish tradition which frowned on graven images was violated by individuals, and especially rich Sephardic Jews or members of the Berlin circle centered around Moses Mendelssohn, but still had great force in the general community. Bit by bit, however, the influence of the Christian environment modified and finally diluted this restriction.

The earliest object in this class can tentatively be called a circumcision medal. It is a product of the Amsterdam Jewish community in the seventeenth century, issued at about the same time as the award to Josef Athias for publishing a fine Hebrew Bible. The Dutch Jews were gaining in prosperity and had taken a role similar to that of the Italian Jews during the Renaissance a century before. A product of this pride in achievement was the 1665 medal ordered by a father on the birth of his son, named David after the beloved king of biblical days. Almost 3½ inches in diameter, and cast and chased in gold, this is the first medal we relate to circumcision.[52] The obverse shows the anointing of David as king, kneeling beside his throne in a palace, and surrounded by a group of nobles and warriors. The style is strongly influenced by the famous Joachimstahl biblical medals issued during the previous century, and like them the legend, entirely in Hebrew, circles the outer rim. The Hebrew reads: "He was born on the fifth day of the month of Tammuz in the year 5425. And the Lord said: 'Arise, anoint him; for this is he!' "[53] The quotation is from 1 Sam. 16:12,

and since the "he" in the quotation refers to the future
King David, it is apparent the medal celebrates the
birth of a son named David. The reference to anointing is further assumed to mean the issuance is associated with the attendant circumcision.

The reverse adds little to the clarification of
the question. King David is shown playing the harp
and dancing before the Ark, which is carried on the
shoulders of four priests. Behind, other priests play
musical instruments; above, the queen looks down
from a Renaissance palace window. In the background can be seen other buildings, portrayed in
Gothic style. The legend on the outer rim, again

First Circumcision Medal
Obverse (slightly enlarged)

entirely in Hebrew, states "And David danced before the Lord with all his might; and David was girded with a linen ephod." The quotation is from 2 Sam. 6:14.

Almost an entire century passed before we have a record of another birth medal, also assumed to celebrate circumcision. This too occurred in Holland. Dated 5508 in Hebrew, and therefore issued in 1747–1748, the obverse of the medal shows a pair of scales with a ribbon, indicating the hope of the parents that later life would deal justly with the child. The reverse is inscribed in Hebrew: "In the city of Dordrecht, Abraham, the son of Hertog [Zangers]." [54]

First Circumcision Medal
Reverse (slightly enlarged)

The next reported circumcision medals come
from the United States. We learn from early Jewish
Americana [55] that two such medals were given to
Jewish fathers. The inscriptions were entirely in
Hebrew. The obverse of the first states, in two circular
lines, "I, Elchanan son of Abraham lifted up my
hands in the holy covenant to circumcise the boy
Moses son of David on Monday, 5 Tishri, this day
being the thirteenth since his birth in 5544." The
second is similar except the name is "Israel son of
Isaac." The mohel issuing the medals was Elchanan
bar Abraham, the two fathers referred to were David
Hays and Isaac Moses, and the year was 1784. Most
interesting, the engraver was Myer Myers, the great
American silversmith who only two years later was
elected chairman of the Gold and Silver Smiths'
Society of New York—and who was also honored by
the presidency of the Spanish and Portuguese Synagogue (Congregation Shearith Israel) of that city in
1759 and again in 1770. There may have been other,
similar medals, for a number on the reverse of one
would seem to indicate a series.

Until recently, it was accepted that the circumcision medal was largely restricted to mid-nineteenth-
century Holland (as well as a few somewhat earlier
by Aaron Kohn of Germany), most of them having
been issued from Utrecht between 1840 and 1870.
The fact that additional medals have been uncovered
going back another two hundred years indicates that
our stereotyped ideas on many Jewish customs must
be revised in accordance with new information. It is
obvious that the Jews extended the Christian baptis-
mal medal to their own custom of circumcision at
a much earlier date than thought. The fragile nature
of these medals and the insecurity of Jewish life
meant they were melted down or destroyed.

The other early medals associated with Jewish
activities were utilitarian in nature. In Amsterdam
the Jewish graveyards were outside the city proper,
and tokens served as an exit permit for the men
who conducted the Jewish funeral processions. Two

from the Ashkenazic community have been preserved at the Jewish Historical Museum in Amsterdam and date from 1671 and 1714. They are of engraved silver with a simple Jewish star and carry inscriptions in Hebrew on both sides. "Let Pass at Muyderbergh" and "Let Pass at Zeeburg" are the pass phrases, according to Dr. Arthur Polak [56]—these being the locations of the cemeteries. On the token dated 1714, the writer has been able to read from a photograph, "The Holy Congregation Amsterdam Ashkenazi"; another photograph (which is not indicated whether from 1671 or 1714) is engraved "In Eternal Memory" and "House of Life," the latter being a euphemism for graveyard. It is not clear whether different passes were issued each year or the later tokens replaced the earlier simply because of wear.

The cemetery of the Portuguese Jews, as distinct from the Ashkenazim, was located at the suburb of Oudekerk, and its picturesque atmosphere attracted seventeenth-century Dutch painters and engravers. There are extant several etchings of the scene. The best-known painting is by J. van Ruysdael, now located at the Dresden Museum. It must be added that the painting bears little relation to reality.

The Amsterdam Chevra Kadisha or Jewish Burial Society also needed permits to bring corpses to the cemeteries. These were likewise in the form of silver tokens, a perforation in the center indicating they were probably stacked on a stick and handed out as required. One dated 1778, now in the National Museum of Israel, shows the city gate with the name of the graveyard at Muyderbergh below and "Let Pass" above—it is significant that the words now, a century later, appear in Dutch rather than Hebrew. However, the reverse, engraved in a double line with a Jewish star, still indicates the date in Hebrew. Another similar token, undated but from the same period, shows a bier on the obverse, while the name "Isac Burgh" replaces the cemetery location. Possibly Isac Burgh was the caretaker.

The other few medals in this category can be

Amsterdam Burial Passes
for Funerals

Amsterdam Passes for Burial
Society Members

Reverse of 1778 Pass
(approximately 1½ times)

Obverse from same period

Jewish Wilhelm School
of Breslau

divided into two groups: school and prize medals, and synagogue medals. Their origins are scattered.

In 1788 the Talmud Torah in London, predecessor to the Jews' Free School, issued a brass plaque, apparently to be worn by the children for identification purposes. It was inscribed "Holy Confraternity of Talmud Torah: Established A. M. 5492." We are indebted for this information to Dr. Cecil Roth.[57] It is apparent that the founding date is merely a guide and that the same plaque might have been worn by a generation of children.

Closely thereafter, in 1808, appears an Italian prize medal, though the city and organization are not indicated. The bronze medal shows a high degree of assimilation, for the words are entirely in Italian, and the inscription—"For Good Conduct of the Brotherhood of Charity and Pity"—is cast in a form entirely Catholic in concept. We are entitled (if only by adoption) to include this as a Jewish award, however, for the date on the edge is engraved in Hebrew, which would be unthinkable, given the time and place, for a Catholic institution.

Properly speaking, the only true medal of this group is the 1791 commemorative medal issued at the foundation of the Jewish Wilhelm School of Breslau. This was the school greatly aided by Lippmann Meyer, for whom, as noted before, a personal medal was issued in 1803. The Breslau Jews, however, were insecure after the anti-Semitic administration of Frederick the Great and judiciously preferred to pay homage to the Christian minister who made possible the existence of the school. On the obverse is shown a new branch growing from a cut trunk with the words "Ennobled by Count Hoym" overhead, and the date, 1791, below. The reverse states "Foundation of the Jewish Wilhelm School at Breslau, the 15th March." The reference is to Count Karl von Hoym, the top minister in the Silesian government, through whom the Jews received a new constitution in 1790.

There are only two synagogue medals struck before the fall of Napoleon,[58] indicating how deeply Jews felt the traditional prohibition when it came to this matter. The first, though we know of it through literary sources, is not listed in any major museum or private collection.[59] Under the impetus of the French Revolution and the formation of the Batavian Republic, a group of the most advanced Ashkenazic Dutch Jews decided to organize a reform synagogue. The Adat Jeshurun Synagogue was inaugurated in Amsterdam in 1800, and a bronze medal was issued to celebrate the occasion. The orthodox tradition of both Sephardic and Ashkenazic elements in Holland was too strong, and the separate congregation lasted only till 1808.

The other synagogue medal commemorates the building of the Bordeaux Synagogue in 1810. The medal is struck in a very simple form, totally different from the rich run of German synagogue medals that follow in the next hundred years—indeed, the dearth of French synagogue medals is quite surprising even into present days. On the obverse, the medal merely states "Consistorial Synagogue of Bordeaux"; on the reverse, "Built in 1810 under the reign of Napoleon the Great." This synagogue was destroyed by a fire in 1873 and replaced by another which, noted for both its size and beautiful interior, still stands and has been called the cathedral synagogue of the Sephardic Jews of France. It may be added that the Bordeaux Jewish community, settled by Marrano refugees, is one of the oldest Jewish groups in France. Under the ambiguous guise of "New Christians"—and with a considerable amount of bribe money at certain occasions—they managed to survive when the Jews of Provence and Paris were dispersed. It is therefore natural that the Bordeaux Jews were the first openly to proclaim the construction of their synagogue.

Bordeaux Synagogue

6. Miscellanea of Jewish Interest

See Catalog for medals cited

MORE THAN A DOZEN medals and tokens from this period fit into no specific group. They are of Jewish interest because they deal with Jewish subjects or persons. They have, however, no central theme.

The earliest and most mysterious Jewish medal —truly, a medallion because of its large size—falls into this category. It is the famed Beer, or Be'er, medal, usually dated 1503, but sometimes 1497, in accordance with the way one reads the Roman numerals. A rather extensive literature has been exclusively devoted to the medal, and yet we are still ignorant of its exact meaning.[60] Even its discovery is cloaked in contradiction; although several authorities affirm the original was found in the Rhone River at Fourvières in the seventeenth century, others maintain it was discovered in the demolition of a synagogue at Lyons in 1654 or 1656. Perhaps there are several original castings. The undisputed original, however, is in the Bibliothèque Nationale at Paris.

The obverse, almost 7 inches in diameter and with a loop for hanging, shows the head of an eminent man facing right and crowned with laurel. Completely encircling the head is a long legend in Hebrew. The style is so mystical that it has been translated in several different ways by scholars such as Leopold Zunz, Louis Loewe, Abraham Geiger, I. Broyde, and, most lately, Arthur Polak. The writer prefers a slightly modified translation of Louis Loewe, given the sense of the medal: "By the decree of Him who is the Guide of the Universe, blessed be He, by His eternal will. When all justice ceased and consideration failed, I beheld the length of that period reaching the appointed end of exile; but reflecting on the ways

Beer Medal
(*slightly reduced*)

of Providence, as by Eli Romi the spiritual traces of them yet remain,[61] (then) I rejoiced and I fully hope in the Redemption, oh eternal, omnipotent God who art great and forgiving."

Beneath the neck is the word "Umilitas" in Latin and its equivalent in Greek, apparently badly written Latin for "humilitas" or our English word "humility." It has further been discovered that the Hebrew legend on the obverse includes, in acrostic form, "Benjamin, son of the learned Rabbi Eliahu Be'er the physician, let him live many good years."

The reverse has a Latin legend on a raised rim. Translated literally, it states: "After darkness, light approaches (since) the last day is judge of happiness." The date is indicated so oddly, as "D.111.M," it is not certain whether the reference is to three years before or after 1500.

We do not know what all this means. At first Benjamin was assumed to be of the important Italian Jewish family of Anau because "humility" can be translated in Hebrew as "ha-anau" or "The Anau." S. Férarès demolished this argument in his careful study, "La médaille dite de Fourvières et sa légende hébraïque," which appeared in the *Revue Numismatique*, Paris, 1910. It is now generally accepted that the family name was Beer, as indicated on the acrostic. The fact that Benjamin Beer refers to his father as Rabbi Elijah the physician contributes little. The leading Jewish physicians in this period often served the papal court, and a little less than a century before, Elijah ben Sabbetai Beer was well known in this capacity. But the time gap is too great between Benjamin and Elijah ben Sabbetai for a father-and-son relation. Leopold Zunz gets around this difficulty by stating the date may not indicate the time of issuance but rather the future time when Benjamin Beer assumed the Messiah would come. Yet it is dangerous to string together such assumptions, and thus the person issuing the medal remains something of an enigma.

We do not even know whom the bust represents. The first interpretation claimed it to be the ninth-century Louis le Debonnaire, who permitted the French Jews to build a synagogue. This theory was soon abandoned. Another body of opinion felt that the figure represented Emperor Augustus, under whose sway the Jews enjoyed freedom from religious persecution. This position is supported by a close resemblance between the bust on the medal and another fifteenth-century medal of Augustus made by Gian Cristoforo Romano of Pisa. But the long hair combed in the "pageboy" style would seem to indicate the head may not represent Augustus, for the coiffure of the early Caesars, though worn long down the neck, was not usually bunched in the back. Another theory is that it commemorated the death of the Spanish Pope Alexander VI and the advent of Julius II, who immediately permitted appeals against judgments of the Inquisition. But this explanation does not tell why the Jews should honor Julius II by adorning a medal with such a distinctly unpopish head unless of course an allusion to a Roman-type emperor would appeal to the Renaissance Pope. And the legends are too messianic in feeling for such an event. Lacking further information, the identity of the bust must remain a question.

What we can surmise, and of most significance, is the state of mind of the Jews at that time as indicated by the medal. The great hope of secular freedom was waning. The Jews had been brutally expelled from France in 1306, massacred in Germany during 1348–49, and subjected to the most appalling pressures in Spain beginning in 1391. The Inquisition in its virulent anti-Jewish form was introduced in 1478. A man as rich and powerful as Isaac Abravanel—whose life span from 1437 to 1508 corresponded with the issuance of the Beer medal—symbolized this loss of faith in the temporal world. Keenly aware from personal experience of the despair gripping the Jewish people, himself a refugee

firstly from Portugal, then Spain, and lastly Naples,
Abravanel devoted his pen to championing the belief
in the Messiah. A portion of a letter he wrote before
fleeing Portugal exemplifies his bitter pessimism with
the world of men:

> From the day that our City was laid in ruins, our
> Temple destroyed and our people exiled, we have
> known neither peace nor respite. The nations
> amongst whom we live do not stop taking council
> and devising means for assailing and harming us;
> and if we do enjoy peace for a brief moment, we
> are soon terrified by frightful news of savage
> persecution against the remnants of Israel coming
> from all corners of the earth. What man subjected
> throughout life to the fear of enemies and the
> strain of distress would grieve when his last hour
> arrives? . . . Weep not for the dying among
> Israel and do not bemoan them! Weep for
> those who are cast from one misfortune to another,
> and for whom God has blocked all avenues of
> relief. For honor has departed from Israel, and
> I wish we were all dead and no more given to
> scorn and derision, to contempt and humiliation.[62]

The Beer medal must be viewed in this context,
for, aside from the details dealing with the identity
of the bust and the acrostic name, the inscriptions
are a paean to redemption through the coming
Messiah. Louis Loewe goes one step further and
postulates that Benjamin Beer was an adherent of
the pseudo-Messiah Asher Lemlein, a contemporary,
and that the words "ELI ROMI" are an abbreviation
of "Asher Lemlein, the Roman Jew"—which makes
sense when we translate literally from the Hebrew,
"E" for Asher, "LI" for Lemlein, "ROM" for Romee
and "I" for yehudi. To support this view it may be
noted that Lemlein, who followed Abravanel in
prophesying the year of 1503 for the Redemption
(precisely the year of the date of the medal)
vanished under seemingly mystical circumstances
the year before. But then again, Lemlein was an
Austrian, not a Roman, Jew. Regardless, this medal
stands among the most important works in Jewish

art history, a testimony to that tragic spiritual with-
drawal caused by unending assault. Without such
evidence, we would not understand much of the
ghetto age that followed.

There are two German medals from the late
seventeenth century which also cannot be properly
categorized. Both have Jewish content, and yet the
writer feels that both were issued by the Christian
community. The first, struck in 1680, is a typical
plague medal, at bottom incantatory in nature, to
ward off the evil spirits that were thought to bring
on the erratic pestilences that swept Europe. The
obverse shows the city of Leipzig. On the reverse
Aaron is depicted holding a censer among the Jews
with a comet, moon, and constellations above; the
legend reads "We have seen the staff of God." Many
similar plague medals were issued, but this is the
only one known by the writer to be solely of Jewish
content.

The other medal (German by style though the
inscription is entirely in Latin), issued in 1696, is
satirically directed against the followers of Sabbetai
Zevi (1626–76), the Turkish-born Jewish pseudo-
Messiah who ultimately converted to Islam. The
medal is adorned with that baroque symbolism so
beloved by a certain German school. The obverse
shows a mountain over which lightning is striking,
while fantastic animals roam at will and an alchemist
plies his trade at a furnace. On the reverse, a lamb
stands holding a banner on a mountain, while a dove
flies overhead carrying an olive branch. The legends
consist of a play on words typical of Christian
Wermuth's medals—though his name is not inscribed
—whereby "Sabbetai" is twisted in mockery with
several biblical quotations referring to the Sabbath.
The quotations are from both the Old and New
Testaments.

Sabbetai Zevi was a disaster for the Jewish
community, but there is nothing in the form of this
medal to indicate it of Jewish origin; rather, the

JEWISH MEDALS

general symbolism and reference to the New Testament can only mean it was struck by a Christian for Christians, indeed with an anti-Semitic approach typical of Christian Wermuth. It is included because of the subject matter.

The last medals of this German group, though struck in 1804 and 1805, have a very modern flavor. They are "calendar medals" issued in Hamburg, showing the days of the week and various holidays; they are thus the ancestors of our present desk calendars and wallet cards serving the same function. Most surprising, the Jewish year and the Jewish holidays are likewise shown. On the obverse the date is marked at the top, followed by "Hamburg. Calend"; the 1805 medal is larger and the last word is spelled out. Beneath is a table which shows the dates of the Sundays of the year, from which the other days can be calculated. On the sides the major Christian holidays are indicated. In the bottom right of the table, the Jewish year is shown—5565 or 5566 —and the date of Rosh Hashanah immediately thereafter. The other Jewish holidays indicated are "Jewish Easter" (Pesach), "Pentecost" (Shavuot), "Destruction" (Tishah Be'Av), "Feast of Reconciliation" (Yom Kippur), and "Tabernacles" (Succot). The reverse has another table indicating the hours when the Hamburg city gates were shut.

The calendar medals were issued by a Hamburg coin dealer by the name of Jobst Schramm, who commissioned the famous Berlin Jew Abraham Abramson to strike them in both gold and silver. The fact they were struck by a Jew does not explain the inclusion of Jewish holidays, for Abramson had to follow the orders of his employer. Rather, we get a clear insight into the importance of Jewish merchants in Hamburg at the time. This free Hansa city did not join the German Confederation until 1815, a decade later. Though the various German civic restrictions applied to the Jews of Hamburg as well, the atmosphere of a major port, the close relation

1804   Hamburg Calendar
Medal

Obverse

to the nearby Dutch cities, and the international
connections of the dominant Sephardic element made
the Jewish commercial presence strongly felt. It must
have been for that reason that the Jewish year and
Jewish holidays were included.

The other medals of this kind are all either
English or Dutch. In Holland, they reflect the internal
life of the Sephardic community.[63] Two are very late
seventeenth-century medals and give a clear view
how these Dutch Jews already were well integrated
into the social and economic structure of that country.
In 1696 Joseph de la Penia (properly Penha), a
shipowner, honored Frans Wiltschut, captain of his
frigate, the *Golden Rock*, with a medal for besting
two French men-of-war off Dunkirk. The obverse
shows a beautiful engraving of the ships at sea, the
reverse the congratulatory inscription. It must be
remembered that in this same period the Italian Jews
were squeezed into ghettos, the German Jews were
in terror of their lives, and the Eastern Jews were
subjected to the most frightful massacres.

Another Dutch medal, also issued in 1696,
shows however that under the skin of official protec-

Joseph de la Penia Honors
His Ship Captain

The Community Leaders Honor
Two Women Poets

tion, the general populace still resented the Jews. A certain David de Pinto (whose family was among the first to settle South Africa for the Dutch) was in danger of having his house sacked by a mob. The militia was called out and saved his property. In gratitude, De Pinto presented the riflemen with engraved six-stiver silver pieces. Two of these specimens are still preserved. Although the contemporary records do not state that the mob was motivated specifically by anti-Semitism, the incident serves as a reminder that even under the best of conditions Jewish life and property were insecure during ·these times.

Nothing more appears in Holland for almost another century. Then in 1786 the *parnassim* (that is, community leaders, in Hebrew) of the Portuguese Jews in Amsterdam gave engraved gold medals to two women poets, Petronella Moens and Adriana van Overstraten, for their poem on Esther. The medals have disappeared, probably long since melted down. It is revealing that the names of the women are pure Dutch, showing already the active cross-cultural pollination existing in Amsterdam at this relatively early date.

The last item from Holland has a more somber background. Issued in 1805, it is more properly a token than a medal and carries with it the smell of the Middle Ages. The obverse indicates the name of the Fishmongers Company of St. Peter's Guild in Amsterdam. The reverse was originally blank, to receive the name of the member. On the one extant, in the private collection of Dr. Arthur Polak of Amsterdam, is engraved, "ALC JOOD," which we know to stand for "Abraham Levi Cohen Jew."

The European guilds, by origin religious, were the labor unions of their time for gifted artists and tradesmen. Most zealous in protecting their privileges, no Jew was allowed entry. The tensions produced in the sixteenth through the eighteenth centuries as a result of this exclusion were remarkably similar to those in present-day America because of the exclu-

Abraham Levi Cohen in the
Amsterdam Fishmongers Company

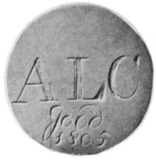

sion of Negroes from such guild unions as plumbers'
and carpenters'. It is for this reason, for example,
we have no good continental European ceremonial
silver before the nineteenth century issued by Jews;
they were forbidden entry into the silversmiths'
guilds.

The Fishmongers was the only Dutch guild which
permitted Jewish entry, provided the word "Jew" was
inscribed after the name. Even here, membership involved certain restrictions, for the Jews were allowed
to sell only in markets specially reserved for them.
The sole guild to let down the barriers, the Fishmongers was also one of the poorest, and it is to be
noted that Abraham Levi Cohen, by the sound of the
name, most probably belonged to the plebeian Ashkenazic Dutch Jews.

The English medals of this group are an odd lot.
Unlike the Dutch medals, which directly reflect the
upward social movement of the Sephardim, they illustrate random activities with no central focus. They
are also later in origin, mainly from the 1780's and
1790's. This is not unexpected, for the English settlement was partly an outgrowth of colonization from
the earlier Dutch community.

The first, issued in 1768, is only incidentally included. A Jewish peddler by the name of Wolf Myers
was robbed and murdered by a man called I. Curtis,
alias Curtel. A medal, one copy of which is now lo-

cated in the private collection of Rabbi Abraham Millgram of Jerusalem, was issued to celebrate the execution of the murderer. Dr. Cecil Roth states that there was another medal made on the same occasion, and both were exhibited in 1944 at the Bodleian Library, Oxford, from the private collection of Sir Arthur Dixon.

1796 Cabbage Society
(*penny size*)

In 1780 a very rare token medal was struck in London in two sizes, corresponding to the English farthing and halfpenny. On the obverse are the words "Cabbage Society," with the depiction in the center of a cabbage or cauliflower. The reverse shows a flower with six petals and around it, in large letters, the word "Purim," with the date. This curious token medal was struck again in 1796, in the English halfpenny, penny, and twopenny sizes, with exactly the same engraving. And still later, in 1814, it appeared again in the twopenny size. In the last issuance, instead of the flower, the reverse shows crossed branches of palm and laurel with berries, and the word "Purim" is not repeated. Some of the 1796 date are also unique in that a slogan has been cut into the milled rims: "An Asylum for the Oppress'd of all Nations."

These pieces have confused the writer more than any others. There is nowhere any literature or explanation founded in solid fact. A key, which at least gives a sensible theory as to their meaning, was discovered in Dalton and Hamer's study of eighteenth-century provincial English token coinage.[64] Under a variant No. 227a, which referred to the slogan on the milled rim of the 1796 variety, there was further reference to another listing. Most astonishing, this turned out to be a medal showing on its obverse the bust of George Washington, while the reverse indicated the arms and crest of the United States, and the words "Liberty and Security." The link between the two items was the slogan, "An Asylum for the Oppress'd of all Nations," shared on the rims.

It seems clear that the Purim token medals belong with the Lord George Gordon series produced by Thomas Spence, which not so coincidentally were also struck between 1780 and 1796. They reflect the social and political turmoil in England incident to the revolt of the American colonies and the French Revolution. As Spence, the rabid believer in the rights of man, engraved on the reverse of a Lord George Gordon token the figure of Cain killing Abel, made explicit by the phrase "The Begining of Oppression," so the engraver of the Purim token medal showed his sympathy with the American Revolution by recalling the biblical story of Purim, of the powerful minister Haman who wanted to oppress a people; and to drive home his point, he put on the rim the same slogan— "An Asylum for the Oppress'd of all Nations"—that appeared on the George Washington medal. This, indeed, was probably the only way an Englishman at that time could condemn George III, the symbolic Haman, without being imprisoned for high treason.

The reason that the 1814 token medal, unlike the 1780 and 1796 varieties, appears without "Purim" is more conjectural. The intervening years had shifted public opinion considerably in England. In 1780, when the fortunes of the American Revolution were at a low point, the issuance of the Purim token medal was an act of defiance against the contemporary Haman, George III. In 1796, the young Napoleon marching through Italy, the heart of clerical and political reaction, seemed the shining knight of freedom to all idealists. But the Napoleon who became an emperor was not the revolutionary leader of 1796. Such radical artists as Beethoven and Shelley, for examples, had come to consider him a new tyrant. It is the cautious judgment of the writer that victory and peace—the crossed branches of palm and laurel— were thus substituted for "Purim" as a result of the defeat of Napoleon in 1814.

There is no attempt to explain the cabbage or cauliflower for the simple reason the writer is at a loss on this point. "The Cabbage Society" might have been

1795   Hackney Promissory
Token
(*halfpenny size*)

one sympathetic to revolution, but we have no record of such a society. Perhaps the cabbage, as a food of the poor, was used as a symbol of the common people, but this is sheer surmise.

We are on firmer ground when we come to the 1795 Rebello token, which indeed has the honor to be considered the first private token ever issued in England. David Alves Rebello was an English Jew of Renaissance proclivities. Though a London businessman, he was an avid student and collector in both the arts and the sciences, turning to numismatics, botany, and art objects with equal avidity. The year before his death, he issued his well-known token. The obverse shows a view of Hackney Church—the private residence of Rebello was at Hackney, near London—with "MCCXC" below, the date 1290 being the year when the church was built. The reverse is dominated by Rebello's initials, "D. A. R.," in script with a wreath of laurel above and encircled by the legend, "Hackney Promissory Token 1795." On the rim is engraved "On demand we promise to pay one penny."

It may be added that Rebello's excellent taste was shown in this token, for he hired as engraver John Milton, medalist at the Royal Mint. The piece was greatly appreciated by collectors and shortly after his death a more mediocre engraver by the name of Jacobs (despite the appellation, not a Jew by known records) made a copy with minor variations.

The writer has reason to believe that the obverse of this token is a copy of a die from another strike. Anthony Durand, in his *Médailles et Jetons des Numismates* (p. 168), indicates that the same obverse appears coupled with another reverse whose legend is "Unite and be free. To persevere is to conquer, 1792," issued in patriotic zeal in relation to the wars between England and France. 1792 obviously precedes 1795. Since the earlier issue is in oval form, Rebello may have been attracted to the design and asked John Milton to repeat it for his token.

In the next year, 1796, J. Rebello (presumably the son) issued a commemorative medal in honor of David Alves Rebello. This is a lovely piece in the English penny size. The obverse again shows Hackney Church, with, however, a portion of the churchyard and several tilted tombstones in the foreground. The reverse is particularly pleasing, showing Father Time leaping forward with a tablet on which the name "David Alves Rebello" is inscribed, decorated to the right with a coin cabinet and to the left with a lyre, globe, and books—obviously alluding to the interests of the departed. Around is the legend "Memoria in Aeterna." John Milton was again the engraver.

A very rare sequel, not recorded in R. C. Bell's exhaustive book on English tokens but located in the collection of the Hebrew Union College at Cincinnati, is a commemorative token issued in turn one year after the death of J. Rebello. Struck in 1804, the obverse has the inscription "Royal Institution" above a crown from which a tree is growing. On the reverse, a large "T" surmounts the words "J A Rebello Esq." The symbolism is obscure aside from the obvious royalist sentiment on the part of the striker, only natural considering the war with Napoleon then raging.

In 1797 appeared a typical merchant's token of the period. The sole reason for its inclusion is that the issuer was Jewish, and this token therefore may be considered the prototype of the flood of trade tokens issued by Jewish concerns throughout the nineteenth century and up to our own time. Struck in English halfpenny size, the obverse shows a view of St. Paul's Cathedral (the issuer's business address was close to St. Paul's); the reverse shows a side view of a weaver at work, with the legend wishing success to the manufacturers of Glasgow. On the edge, it states "Payable at M. & H. Oppenheims Toy Warehouse London." We will never know whether this advertising stunt induced the visitors from Glasgow to buy toys from Messrs. Michael and Harry Oppenheim.

The last items to be considered have a certain

1796 Rebello Commemorative
(*penny size*)

1797 First Known Jewish
Merchant's Token
(*slightly reduced*)

importance because they indicate that the dying days of the eighteenth century already involved global conflicts which included Jews. The English and French contest for world domination spread to India, where the French had been supplanted somewhat earlier. Napoleon, whose Egyptian campaign was directed toward India, was busy encouraging native revolt. Tipu of Mysore, discontent under his vassalage, rose against the British with French encouragement. Colonel Arthur Wellesley, to be known later as the Duke of Wellington, sent in a mixed English and Indian force, and took Seringapatam, the capital of Mysore. A bronze medal for distinguished service in this action was given to Samuel Ezekiel Kharcelkar, of the auxiliary forces. Kharcelkar was a Bene Israel, of the native Indian Jews who had settled very early on the western coastline of India. The medal shows on the obverse the British lion subduing the tiger of Sultan Tipu, with Arabic inscription, and the English date of May 4, 1799. The reverse indicates the troops moving up for the assault of Seringapatam, with Persian inscription and the Mohammedan date, 27th Zilkad, A. H. 1213. The medals were issued in a general run, without specific inscription of name, and were also awarded in gold, silver, and tin. This specific medal, which was exhibited at the famous Anglo-Jewish Historical Exhibition at the Royal Albert Hall of London in 1887, is presently unlocatable.

In this same class is a silver war medal issued for volunteers by the Danes, who were allied with Napoleon in the 1801 defense of Copenhagen against the victorious English attack led by Nelson. One of these medals was awarded to Melchior Heymann, "of the Jewish Congregation"; his name is punched on the rim. Heymann was listed as No. 10 on the blockade ship *Jylland* (*Jutland*). The medal is in the personal collection of the well-known Danish numismatist and dealer Johan Chr. Holm.

7. Exclusions

See Catalog for medals cited

THE QUESTION of what to exclude from a listing of early Jewish medals might entail as much space as the actual listing. These exclusions fall into natural categories.

Marrano names that appear in a Christian context are not admitted. From the end of the fourteenth century masses of Jews, with varying degrees of sincerity, converted to the Catholic religion in Spain. In most cases they adopted pure Spanish appellations. Names of old Christians, thus, are inseparably mixed with those of sincere new Christians and also with those of Marranos who continued a secret adherence to Judaism. The best scholarship is balked by this problem: for example, in the Carvajal family, all three conditions are mixed within a few generations. Judging by the context, I have excluded medals for men like Cardinal Bernardino Carvajal, Pedro Alvarez de Toledo, Antonio de Santamaría, María de Rojas, Iñigo López de Mendoza, Francisco de Mendoza, Juan de Mendoza, and Juan Bautista Villanova. As noted before, the case of Gonzalo Pérez is on the border. Another medal excluded is that of Alonso Pimentel, cast in 1562. (See Armand III, 283, M, Anon.) The Marrano side of the Carvajal family married with the Pimentel family, but the writer has been unable to find out more. The only doubtful case included is that of Antonio González, previously mentioned, for the circumstances of his Marrano background seem quite clear.

Insofar as French Marranos are concerned, Michel de Montaigne might be included, for we know that his mother, Antonia Lópes, was definitely of Marrano extraction. (Her sister, Ursula Lópes, has been medalized; see the 1555 and 1580 listings under "Marranos and Christian Converts.") There is even some question about Montaigne's paternal ancestry, for the great Spanish writer Americo Castro states that his father, of Portuguese descent, was probably also Jewish. But no medals of Montaigne can be found from the period, though Gatteaux struck one in 1817, Godel in 1821, and the French Medal Mint issued a fourth centenary medal in 1933 honoring the noted essayist.

Michel de Nostre-Dame, better known by his Latinized name of Nostradamus, also would be eligible. This famous astrologer and maker of prophecies was not only Jewish by origin on both sides but, clearly aware and proud of the fact, claimed that his prophetic powers derived by descent from "the tribe of Issachar." In fact, at one point Nostradamus had to flee Provence owing to certain irreverent remarks about the Virgin. Yet the writer has been unable to discover any medal issued for Nostradamus in the period surveyed.

The Portuguese Marrano picture is simpler. Two sixteenth-century Marranos from that country have been memorialized on stamps: Pedro Núñez, the royal cosmographer to King João III; [65] and Garcia da Orta, a physician and botanist. Neither appears on any medallic listing.

It is rather curious that no Spanish or Portuguese Inquisition medals exist depicting Jews either in penitence or being burned at an auto-da-fé. With the strong Iberian artistic tradition, we might expect such representations. One explanation may be that Spanish and Portuguese medals have not yet been so finely classified and cataloged as those in other Western European countries.[66]

The case of Italy during the Renaissance is more documented. Bernardo di Lutozzo Nasi and his son Ruberto di Bernardo Nasi, despite the famous Jewish name of Nasi, were Christians.[67] I have also, perhaps arbitrarily, excluded all medals with the names Rossi and Fiorentino, though the former is a most ancient Jewish name in Italy while the latter was

The Bohemian Christian Reformer Huss at the Stake

borne by a great Italian Jewish poet. There is no evidence that Giovanni Antonio de' Rossi, or Adriano and Giovanni Fiorentino, all renowned Renaissance medalists, were of Jewish origin. Excluded likewise is Niccolo Fiorentino, another Renaissance medalist, whose real name was Niccolò di Forzore Spinelli.

The German Renaissance produces problems as well. So-called Jewish names are often old German names adopted less than two centuries ago. When we search back, there is an impulse wrongly to assume men with these names to have been Jewish. Hans Schwartz, a very great sixteenth-century Nürnberg medalist, did a uniface portrait of Kunz von der Rosen. In reality, Rosen was the confidential councillor of Maximilian I. Matthes Gebel in 1529 did a medal of Jakob Heller von der Haimen. Joachim Deschler just slightly later made medallic portraits of Albrecht von Rosenberg, Marquart von Stein, and Wratislaw von Bernstein. In 1562 Hans Wild portrayed Tobias Stern, and in 1579 the Master of Eichhorn did the same for Abraham Gruenberg. Sixteenth-century medals were issued for Jakob Philipp Adler, S. Jakob Marcus, as well as several Germans (and a Dutchman) with the surname Joachim.

This is true elsewhere in the eighteenth century. A medal was struck in 1773 for a Swedish doctor by the name of Nicolas von Rosenstein. The court doctor for Gustav III of Sweden, Abraham Baeck, was honored by a medal in 1797. A Russian doctor, G. von Asch, was medalized in 1770. Not one of these men was a Jew according to any known records.

An entirely separate category of exclusion is the Christian medal inscribed with Hebrew. The Renaissance fostered a new interest in the Hebrew language as part of the classical trinity of Latin, Greek, and Hebrew. Many medals of the period thus bear Hebrew words or legends without any reference to Judaism. Giovanni Boldú, for example, a fifteenth-century Venetian medalist, signed his name in Hebrew, as well as in Latin and Greek, on certain of his medals.

90

Giovanni Boldú—Self-Portrait
with Name in Hebrew
and Greek

Jesus Medal with Hebrew

A sixteenth-century Genoese nobleman by the name of Battista Spinola de Serravalis was medalized. The reverse of the medal shows a ship in the midst of a storm with a legend in Hebrew: "Save me, Lord, I entreat You." [68] Pope Pius V had a Hebrew legend put on the reverse of one of his papal medals. Portrait medals of Christ were often engraved with the name of Jesus in Hebrew; some even have entire inscriptions in Hebrew as well. Though rarer, the same is true for medals showing Mary and Joseph.

In fact, very many commemorative medals from Protestant countries were adorned in Hebrew with "JHVH," beginning in the sixteenth century. Certain Protestant kings, especially Charles IX and Gustave II (Gustavus Adolphus) of Sweden, and Christian IV of Denmark, often engraved both coins and medals the same way. All these examples obviously have nothing to do with a catalog of Jewish medals.

Mention has been made of the anti-Semitic medals of Christian Wermuth. Some writers, including C.

1634 Death Commemorative
for Gustavus Adolphus
of Sweden

Coronation Medal of Henry
VIII of England

Fieweger, Dr. Antoine Feill, and M. J. Meissner,[69]
claim that certain medals of Wermuth classed as
"Hahnrei" or "Satyric-Erotic" are likewise anti-
Semitic. Typical subjects are a stag with long horns,
a man with horns on his head riding on a cock, a
child mounted on a stag, and a crane with a man's
face on the breast. The sole reason they are assumed
anti-Semitic is that similar inscriptions to the Feder
Jude medals are also found on these, particularly referring to cuckolding. But, in the opinion of the
writer, this is inconclusive evidence. No Jews are
represented nor are any inscriptions specifically relating to Jews. Christian Wermuth was a general
satirist who issued the enormous number of some
thirteen hundred pieces—many executed by his students, including his two sons—and he poked ven-
omous fun in all directions. The confusion regarding
these medals is more probably due to the use of hybrid dies. In this same category, also attributed to
Wermuth, is a medal categorized by Moritz Stern as

Satiric Medal on John Law's
Schemes, Formerly Thought
Anti-Semitic

anti-Semitic in his catalog of the former Berlin Jewish Museum.[70] On the obverse it shows two gentlemen with pikes whispering together, the inscription overhead in German being "Money is the watchword." The reverse shows a man labeled a Jew by Stern, holding a torn purse with money falling out; the inscription continues "As it comes, so it goes." According to Max Bernhart (in his *Medaillen und Plaketten*, p. 78), this medal is a very early eighteenth-century satire on John Law's financial schemes at the French court after the death of Louis XIV.

A similar ambiguous category refers to Johann Christian Reich, the anti-Semitic medalist who struck the later 1772 Korn Judes. In that same year he issued tokens of like size representing the biblical Joseph as a benefactor. The obverses show Joseph while his brothers kneel before him. The reverses list the high prices of food, as do the Korn Judes. Obviously issued to warn against hoarding, they cannot be considered specifically anti-Semitic.

Biblical medals, including those Jewish in origin, are likewise excluded. The purpose of this study is to include only contemporary material. The Old Testament was a favorite subject for medalists, and Italian Renaissance plaquettes in particular are adorned with such themes. This was also true north of the Apennines. One of the best known medals of Lorenz Rosenbaum, a sixteenth-century Swiss medalist,[71] is Judith, showing that biblical lady holding a sword and the head of Holofernes. The very great German medalist Hans Reinhart the Elder, working 1535 to 1568, did biblical medals, including Old Testament pieces such as Moses and the Burning Bush, Abraham's Sacrifice of Isaac, and Jonah and the Whale. His medals so inspired Central Europe, they led to a whole new school that imitated the technique, the "Joachimstahl" group from Bohemia.[72] Most Joachimstahl medals have an Old Testament theme on one side and a complementary New Testament theme on the other. Some, however, depict only

Hans Reinhart: Moses and the
Burning Bush

Obverse

Joachimstahl: Jacob's Dream
by Wolf Milicz

Joachimstahl: Moses Medal,
Thought "Jewish"

Old Testament themes, and these, which occasionally include knowledgeable Hebrew legends, are often reported by enthusiastic amateurs as "Jewish" medals.

In the seventeenth and early eighteenth centuries interest continued in Old Testament themes. Hans Krauwinkel of Nürnberg—whose work consists of jetons rather than medals—struck a series with subjects such as David and Jonathan, Saul and Samuel, Joab and Amasa, Samuel and David, and Mordechai and Haman. In imitation of the Joachimstahl technique, he also juxtaposed themes, one on each side. Adam and Eve are contrasted with Christ on the Cross; and Judith, sword in hand, is complemented by the virtuous Roman matron Lucretia stabbing herself.[73] Christian Maler of Nürnberg portrayed a covetous David staring at a naked Bathsheba, as well as David Playing the Harp. Wermuth, who has often been mentioned before, also put his hand to biblical themes such as David and Bathsheba, King Solomon in the Temple, Joseph and Potiphar's Wife, Jacob and the Angel, the Prophet Jonah and the Prophet Elijah.

David and Jonathan by Philipp
Heinrich Mueller

Krauwinkel's Imitation of the
"Judaea Capta" Coin

The Old Testament was a burning subject in those
centuries so filled with religious strife, and the great
contemporaneous graphic art often served as models
for such medalists. Related to these are the so-called
Friendship Medals, usually based on the Old Testament. Wermuth portrayed David and Jonathan together. Georg Hautsch from Nürnberg depicted
Rachel and Ruth, as well as Joseph and Daniel.
Philipp Heinrich Mueller from Augsburg did David
and Jonathan and also the rather unusual combina-
tion of Jacob and Esau. It must be kept in mind
that pietistic Protestants in this period, reacting
against the bureaucratic structure of the Catholic
church, went back to the Old Testament for inspira-
tion that was wholly Christian in sentiment. This attitude was especially true in Bohemia, with its mili-
tant Hussite tradition.

A maverick group excluded are the so-called
Prague Jewish medals of the early seventeenth century. We know that Jakob Bassevi was involved in
money schemes at Prague at this time with both
Jewish and Christian partners. Apparently there were
Jewish goldsmiths operating in Bohemia as well,
though their activities were illegal, for no Jew was
allowed to join the guild. Precisely at this period a
number of large, thin gold medals were issued at
Prague, bearing portraits of eminent personalities
like Constantine the Great, Charlemagne, Louis XII
of France, and Henry VII of England. Owing to this
coincidence, Johann David Kohler assumed that
Prague Jewish goldsmiths were the medalists. But Max
Bernhart, the late curator of the Munich Coin Collection, has established that there is no evidence
pointing to this assumption, and it would seem proper
to exclude the thesis.[74]

A few interesting private English tokens from
the late eighteenth century have also been eliminated,
though here ignorance rather than error is the reason.
At Birmingham in 1798 a penny token was struck by
a certain Benjamin Jacob. The obverse shows a very
heavy-nosed gentleman holding a pair of scales over

a counter surrounded by miscellaneous objects. On
the reverse we read "B.N. Jacob Auctioneer Iron-
monger &c." Though the assembly of facts seems to
indicate the gentleman was Jewish, there is no proof.[75]
Another tradesman's token from this same period is
equivocal. The obverse shows a Gothic tower with the
words "Evesham Penny." The reverse is adorned
with a cypher, "TT" (standing for Thomas Thompson) and "Payable by June 6, 1796." There is
nothing Jewish about this token, except that R. C.
Bell in his *Tradesmen's Tickets and Private Tokens
(1785–1819)* adds an explanatory note: "Thomas
Thompson was the illegitimate son of Mr. Levi, a
well known collector of tokens" (p. 195).

Superimpositions or cuttings into coins are likewise excluded. In the Jewish Museum of New York
we have several excellent examples. A German copper
pfennig dated 1760 has the name "Bilba Hendlhin"
cut into the reverse in Hebrew letters. Another
example is the name "David Fernbach" cut in Hebrew
letters into the reverse of a Polish groshen of King
Stanislaus August, who reigned from 1764 to 1796.
These are intriguing but cannot legitimately be
included.

Medals by Jewish artists on non-Jewish subjects
are likewise eliminated. Jacob Abraham and his son,
Abraham Abramson, were very renowned eighteenth-

Jacob Abraham Medal on Non-Jewish Subject for 500th
Anniversary of the State of Königsberg 1755

century medalists. Their medals dealing with Jewish subjects are included, while those with non-Jewish subjects are excluded. No medals dealing with Jewish subjects are known by such eighteenth-century medalists as Salomon Aaron Jacobson, Samuel Judin, Abraham Aaron, Abraham Jacobs, and Abraham Heilbut. The same is true for the renowned Jean Henri Simon, engraver to Louis XVI and, later, to King William I, who ruled over Belgium. Nor have medals of Jews from this period been included if they were struck in a much later period. Several excellent medals, for example, have been issued of Spinoza in more recent times.

Coins by Jewish mint masters are obviously excluded, though Jewish participation in this trade has long and honorable roots. The history of Hebrew on medieval denars and bracteates—both the names of the mint masters and actual Hebrew words and legends—is a fascinating but different subject from the present one.

Abraham Abramson Medal
on Non-Jewish Subject—
Vaccination Medal, with
Frederick William III of Prussia
on obverse

Obverse   *Reverse*

False shekels and half shekels, imaginary and counterfeit, also are an intriguing but separate field of study. Though some may have been issued by Jews,[76] the vast majority were made by German and Bohemian Christians for sale as souvenirs on pilgrimage to Jerusalem or to religious centers such as the replica of the Holy Sepulchre erected at the city of Goerlitz in eastern Germany. Nor have the Holy City of Jerusalem "imitation coins," inscribed in Hebrew and possibly issued as early as the fifteenth century under unknown circumstances, been included.[77] Although they refer on the reverses to Abraham and Sarah, David and Solomon, to Joshua and Mordechai, it is only conjecture to consider them Jewish in origin. Medals by Christians about Christian activity in Palestine are likewise excluded, such as the several struck in 1799 by the English to commemorate Admiral Sidney Smith's repulsion of Napoleon's attacks against the city of Acre.

The distinction between medals on the one hand, and certain tokens, jettons, and amulets on the other, is often difficult to make. Included are tokens where the engraving is so fine they may almost be considered in the class of medals. Also I have included certain tokens which illustrate Jewish events or personalities. All tokens for charity, ritual slaughter, electioneering, and use as small change are excluded.

I have had great trouble in trying to establish correct sizes in millimeters. This is due to several reasons. The first is that metal shrinks when cooling, and later castings tend to drop in size one or two millimeters, with still later castings being even smaller. Many of these medals have been recast, and thus the original size may be the largest when the variants are close. Furthermore, it is quite easy to make a mistake of a millimeter when measuring, particularly when the medal is worn. But the most serious problem is that certain of these medals, and especially ones of early date, have disappeared. I have often, therefore, had to rely on former source

Typical False Shekels

(*approximately 1½ times*)

Holy City of Jerusalem
"Imitation Coin"

Obverse
(*reverses vary*)

98

Ritual Slaughter Token, Italian
"Large Chicken"—3 Baiocco
(*approximately 2 times*)

Electioneering Token
"Yes" Vote

material rather than on direct examination, and unfortunately it is quite apparent that textual misprints were common. The pattern of theft is so evident during the Hitler period insofar as sixteenth- and seventeenth-century medals are concerned, that I am convinced many will reappear within fifty years.

Another technical problem is the distinction among tin, lead, and pewter medals. German catalogs often use the terms for tin and pewter interchangeably. The three metals are labeled without clarity elsewhere as well. "White metal" is sometimes used by English sources when they are not sure whether the content is poor silver or another alloy. Indeed, in old medals, discolored by age, it is difficult to establish precisely the type of metal used. I have therefore followed the path of convenience and used the definitions from source, knowing in many cases the same medal probably is labeled differently.

It should be emphasized that the writer does not pretend to have exhausted the subject. The Bibliography lists relevant sources; but for every listing, there were several others examined with negative results. Some three hundred letters were sent out to various museums and significant collections. Yet some material undoubtedly slipped by.

It stands to reason that many sources with uncataloged material, or whose private files were not available, possess additional items. As an example, the 1687 Christian Wermuth satirical medal "The Pharisee, Risen from Death" was illustrated in a recent reissue of Dr. Max Bernhart's *Medaillen und Plaketten* (revised by Tyll Kroha in 1966). I wrote to the publishers inquiring as to its source and received no answer. New material will keep cropping up and will be integrated with what we now know as the result of additional research. This volume, therefore, can be considered as merely the latest compilation of our present knowledge.

Notes

1. *Anti-Semitic Medals*

1. Eduard Fuchs, *Die Juden in der Karikatur* (Munich: Albert Langen, 1921), p. 206.

2. A few students of the subject believe the first Korn Jude medal was issued in 1624. In the opinion of the writer, this is due to the fact that the old German "9" looks very much like "2," especially on a worn surface. The late authorities Dr. Bruno Kisch and Dr. Bruno Kirschner agree with the writer in excluding 1624. See *CIBA Symposia*, Jan.–Feb., 1948 for Dr. Kisch's view and item no. 26B in Bibliography for that of Dr. Kirschner.

3. See item no. 36 in Bibliography. The specific medal is discussed under item no. 30 of Pfeiffer's listing.

4. See item no. 32 in Bibliography. Dr. Bruno Kirschner (see item no. 26B in Bibliography) states that Johann Buchheim, who lived in Silesia during the latter part of the seventeenth century, also struck Korn Judes. His source of information is not clear.

5. For a brief but excellent study of this problem, see Selma Stern, *The Court Jew* (Philadelphia: Jewish Publication Society of America, 1950), pp. 162–76.

6. Dr. Bruno Kirschner, on p. 44 of item no. 26B in Bibliography, states that several Feder Judes were made by Christian Wermuth around 1650. This is impossible for the obvious reason that Wermuth was born in 1661.

7. Dr. Bruno Kirschner, item no. 26B in Bibliography, states that two other medalists, J. Blum and Reteke, issued some of these Feder Judes. An auction catalog of Karl Kress from Munich (107th Auction, item no. 1631) is his source regarding Reteke. His source on Blum is not clear. Johann Christoph Reteke was a late-seventeenth-century medalist at Hamburg. Johann Blum, whose active period from 1631 to 1660 would seem to exclude him as a striker of these medals, resided at Bremen.

8. See p. 41 of item no. 26B in Bibliography. The source material is not clear.

9. See item no. 17 in Bibliography. Reference is to Catalog No. 3438. Several writers on this subject, of German birth, have confused the matter by translating Feill's word "zwitter" as "hermaphrodite," the first usage of the word in German-English dictionaries. "Zwitter" without doubt stands for "mongrel" (of hybrid dies), the secondary translation of the German word.

10. See item no. 40 in Bibliography.

11. See pp. 40, 41, and 43 of item no. 26B in Bibliography.

12. In country districts a "feather merchant" is used to mean salesmen

who sell shoddy goods. They are light like feathers and hence have little value. This might be a related meaning, carried over from folk thought of earlier days. It should also be noted that in the period at question Jews were often peddlers.

13. *Hamburgische Münzen und Medaillen,* Vol. II, p. 22, no. 12.

14. See item no. 48 in Bibliography. The medal is listed as number 224.

15. See p. 35 of item no. 26B in Bibliography.

16. The fire was supposedly the result of cabalistic experiments on the part of Rabbi Naphtali Cohen from Lublin.

17. See item no. 39 in *The Coin Cabinet,* published by The Historical Museum of Frankfurt am Main, Oct.–Dec. 1964.

18. A fascinating account of the entire story is given by Dr. Curt Elwenspoek, *Jew Süss Oppenheimer* (London: Hurst & Blackett, Ltd., 1931).

19. See p. 50 of item no. 26B in Bibliography.

2. *Marranos and Christian Converts*

20. The date would appear to be 1515, yet in all but one source is listed as 1518.

21. See item no. 21A in Bibliography on the Antwerp Marrano community.

22. An eighteenth-century copy of this medal, in coppered lead, exists in the collection of Herbert J. Erlanger, New York City.

23. The Latin indicated is Bvrchardo. Some sources translate this as Bernhard rather than Burckhardt.

24. This information comes from the old records of the County Museum of Heidelberg. Some doubt can be registered by careful scrutiny of the photographs of the medal.

25. Most sources consider Mengs of Jewish origin, at least on the paternal side. According to Julius Margolinsky, Librarian of the Jewish Community in Copenhagen, this is not backed by evidence. Ismael Mengs, the father, was born in Copenhagen before Jews settled in that city, and the name of Mengs has never been known as Jewish in Denmark.

3. *The Slow Rise of Jewish Emancipation*

26. For a detailed account of this period, see Otto Muneles, ed., *Prague Ghetto in the Renaissance Period* (Prague: The State Jewish Museum in Prague, 1965).

27. Actually, the medal is based on premature rejoicing. It was not until September 1748 that a small group of Jews were allowed to return. They had to pay to the Queen's treasury the enormous sum of 240,000 florins for this act of grace.

28. La Médaille, 11 Quai de Conti, Paris VI, France.

29. Dr. Arthur Polak (p. 33 of item no. 40 in Bibliography) puts the matter succinctly: "In his own grand way, Napoleon wanted to promote the Jews to citizenship and thus make them conscripts."

30. It is a matter of interest that Jean Henri Simon, engraver to Louis XVI and one of the most renowned Jewish medalists of this period, became a colonel in the Napoleonic army.

4. *Medals Commemorating Individual Jews*

31. For the best study of the Jews in this period, see pp. 153–228 of item no. 43 in Bibliography. See also Cecil Roth, *The Jews in the Renaissance* (New York: Harper and Row, 1965).

32. A small capital "P" is stamped on the lower part of the sleeve, almost lost in the folds: it is actually seen more clearly extruded in reverse position on the other side. A minority school deems this letter to stand for another medalist, Giovanni Paolo Poggini. Other sources claim this medal to have been issued in 1556 or 1557. However, Paul Grunebaum-Ballin in *Joseph Naci, duc de Naxos* (Paris, 1968), definitely establishes the birth date as 1540 and the medal itself states Gracia Nasi was eighteen at the time.

33. It is a little-known fact, but the great-grandmother of the violently anti-Semitic Ferdinand was reputed to be a Jewess. Many Marranos had high hopes at the beginning of his reign because of this. See "Ferdinand and Isabella," *The Jewish Enclyclopedia* (New York and London: Funk and Wagnalls Company, 1907), Vol. 5.

34. The 1503 Beer medal, which will be discussed later, is too cryptic to be considered a personal medal.

35. David Abarbanel Lindo of this family was a relative of the mother of Benjamin Disraeli and performed the initiatory rite at the circumcision of the later prime minister of England.

36. See pp. 54–59, 195–201, 210, 211, 287–93, and 295–99 of item no. 38 in Bibliography. Also Harold Soref, "Anglo-Jewish Grandees," *The Menorah Journal* (Autumn–Winter 1957).

37. Information from 1957.

38. See p. 60 of item no. 45 in Bibliography.

39. See pp. 239 and 240 of item no. 13 in Bibliography.

40. The Kaullas were an old and well-connected German Jewish family. It is of interest to note that the late Fritz E. Oppenheimer, international lawyer and special assistant to General Lucius D. Clay, the American Military Governor in Germany after World War II, was married to Elsbeth Kaulla. Fritz E. Oppenheimer, born in Berlin, was the son of Ernst Oppenheimer and Amalie Friedlaender. In our time, three powerful German Jewish families, all mentioned in this early catalog of Jewish medals, conjoined.

41. See item no. 26 in Bibliography.

42. For the best picture of this period, see Marvin Lowenthal, *The Jews of Germany* (Philadelphia: Jewish Publication Society of America, 1936), pp. 197–216. Also Selma Stern, *op. cit.*

43. A purist might include a fourth medal in this group, a memorial struck by Abramson for Gotthold Ephraim Lessing in 1781. Lessing, of course, was not a Jew. On the reverse, however, at the base of a funeral urn, appears "Nathan der Weise," the title of the famous play in which the author depicts with great sympathy the position of the Jews. The character of Nathan the Wise was modeled on Moses Mendelssohn.

44. Dr. Bruno Kirschner (see p. 72 of item no. 26B in Bibliography) states that this medal might be a "funny mint fake" issued as a joke between Frederick the Great and his mint master Ephraim.

45. Though outside the province of this work, a medal was issued in 1870 memorializing Franchetti's heroic death.

46. See p. 64 of item no. 45 in Bibliography.

47. See pp. 109–11 of item no. 6 in Bibliography.

48. See p. 79 of item no. 45 in Bibliography.

49. Dating from 1749, a famous English satire entitled "The Jerusalem Infirmary" poked fun at the Beth Holim, a hospital in London which was restricted to "the poor professing the Portuguese Jewish Religion." The engraving is extremely witty. See item No. 295 in *Anglo-Jewish Portraits* by Alfred Rubens.

50. See p. 15 of item no. 21 in Bibliography.

51. An early sixteenth-century Italian Jewish medalist by the name of Moses da Castellazzo was reported to have made a medallion of Ercole I, Duke of Ferrara. See Cecil Roth, *The Jews in the Renaissance, op. cit.*, p. 192. But no work of this man survives. Excluded also are various folk pieces, amulets, and the like.

5. *Medals Commemorating Jewish Activities*

52. It should be noted that the Strauss-Rothschild Collection, now located in the Cluny Museum of Paris, contains a circumcision bowl attributed to the sixteenth century. The jump from a bowl to a medal apparently took a century in the Christian environment of Western Europe.

53. The writer has seen the medal only in photographs and is indebted to Dr. Isaiah Shachar, Curator of the Department of Jewish Art in the Israel National Museum, Jerusalem, for filling in certain points.

54. The medal was cataloged by Dr. Horatio R. Storer as No. 4182 in his *Medicina in Nummis* (see item no. 49 in Bibliography).

55. Vol. II of the Lyons Collection, p. 383, American Jewish Historical *Society*, No. 27, 1920.

56. See item no. 39 in Bibliography, each token-medal listed according to its date.

57. See p. 20 of item no. 21 in Bibliography.

58. A rather cryptic reference is made to what might be a very early synagogue medal in the Strauss-Rothschild Collection at the Cluny Museum of Paris. Some of the medals in this collection were described by Moise Schwab in an article appearing in the *Revue des Etudes Juives*, Vol. 23 (1891–92), pp. 136–38. Schwab refers to a medal "probably in commemoration of the inauguration of a synagogue," whose description is that of a temple "rather Greek than Oriental," with legends about King Solomon. The piece is reputedly from the sixteenth or seventeenth century. Since the legends are in French and the building shown admittedly cannot be identified, it is only conjecture to suppose this is a Jewish synagogue medal.

59. See p. 23 of item no. 39 in Bibliography.

6. *Miscellanea of Jewish Interest*

60. L. A. Mayer, *Bibliography of Jewish Art* (Jerusalem: The Magnes Press, Hebrew University, 1967), lists nine items alone in the Index. Also see pp. 25 and 26 of item no. 40 in Bibliography. Also p. 12 of item no. 21, where there is an error in the Latin quoted.

61. That is to say, God ordained the Romans to permit Jews to exist as a testimonal to the coming Messiah.

62. A letter to Yehial of Pisa, written on October 4, 1482. Quoted in B. Netanyahu, *Don Isaac Abravanel Statesman and Philosopher* (Philadelphia: The Jewish Publication Society of America, 1953), p. 29.

63. The only complete study of Jewish medals of any one country is that of Dr. Arthur Polak, dealing with Holland. See item no. 39. This book has an abbreviated English translation and is essential for all interested in the subject.

64. See p. 118 of item no. 14 in Bibliography.

7. Exclusions

65. There is a bronze oval medal, 44 x 34 mm, of Pedro Núñez. But this must be a different person, for he is specifically referred to as a Spanish goldsmith. See Francisco Alvarez-Ossorio, No. 411. It is of some interest to note that cosmographer Núñez's grandchildren were seized by the Inquisition.

66. There is a medal (in several varieties) of John Huss, the early fifteenth-century Bohemian religious reformer and martyr, whose reverse clearly shows Huss, naked and bound, being burned at the stake. This medal is relatively common. Huss, of course, was not a Jew.

67. Heiss states that Ruberto Nasi "was probably of Jewish origin, Nasi signifying *prince* in Hebrew." See p. 150 of item no. 22A in Bibliography, "Florence et les Florentins," Première Partie. Cecil Roth, the noted authority on Italian Jewry, has found no factual evidence to support this conclusion based on false analogy.

68. Armand II, 209, 30 (see item no. 3 in Bibliography).

69. See item nos. 17, 20, and 32 in Bibliography.

70. See p. 57 of item no. 48 in Bibliography.

71. Despite the sound of the name, Rosenbaum was a Christian. Sixteenth- and seventeenth-century Germany was filled with Christian medalists and mint masters with Jewish-sounding names. A perusal of Forrer's *Biographical Dictionary of Medallists* will acquaint the readers with names by the score—with their variants—such as Jacob, Kaplan, Siegel, Schwartz, Roth, Stein, Schoenfeld, Blum, Weiss, and Rosenberg. Not one of these men was Jewish according to known records.

72. The finest study of Joachimstahl medals is by Viktor Katz, *Die erzgebirgische Prägmedaille des XVI Jahrhunderts* (Prague, 1931).

73. Krauwinkel was also one of the first men to start imitating classical Jewish coins. He did an imitation of the "Judaea Capta" coin issued by the Romans, showing the bust of Vespasian on the obverse and "Ivdaea Capta, S.C." on the reverse. These confused numismatists for some time.

74. See item no. 7 in Bibliography.

75. See p. 172 of item no. 6 in Bibliography.

76. The earliest dated shekel was incorrectly assumed to have been minted by Mordecai Meisel, the great sixteenth-century leader of the Jewish community of Prague. The piece, dated 1584, is in fact a cast of an older medal which may or may not have been connected with Prague Jewry. See Bruno Kisch, "Shekel Medals and False Medals," in *Historia Judaica*, Vol. III (Oct. 1941), p. 87. Also see items no. 25 in Bibliography and Sir George Hill, *Becker the Counterfeiter* (London: Spink & Sons, 1955), reprint. It is also of interest that Johann Buchheim, who may have struck some of the anti-Semitic Korn Judes, is the only known medalist to have signed (with his initials, I.B.) a false shekel.

77. See item no. 34 in Bibliography (volume is in Hebrew). Their origin may look to the Rabbis of the Talmud (Babli, Baba Kama 97b) who refer to a coin struck with the image of "David and Solomon on one side and Jerusalem the Holy City on the other side."

Catalog of Medals

1. *Anti-Semitic Medals*

1670   300th Anniversary of the alleged Desecration of the Host at Enghien. Obverse, the Holy Sacrament; reverse, inscription. Belgian celebration of the burning alive of Jews in 1370 on the pretext of their having profaned the consecrated wafer. This medal was issued again on the 450th anniversary, in 1820.

> *39 mm; silver and copper*

> Last cataloged in the Hamburger Museum für Völkerkunde, Hamburg
> Listed in Moritz Stern's *Aus dem Berliner Jüdischen Museum.* This collection disappeared under the Nazis.

1670   Same, except reverse is an escutcheon and size is

> *32 mm*

> Listed in Moritz Stern's *Aus dem Berliner Jüdischen Museum.* This collection disappeared under the Nazis.

1686   Participation of the Jews, with the Turks, in the defense of Buda against the Christian attack. Austrian. Medal refers to Ofen, old German name for Buda, now Budapest. Obverse, a smelting furnace, with Turk and Jew inserting metal and legend accusing Turks and Jews of making money out of the war; reverse, inscription stating luck has been against Mohammed and the money cannot even be used to save the city.

> *41, 43, or 44 mm; silver, bronze, and tin; Martin Brunner, though name of engraver is not on medal (also listed as 47 mm in Albert Wolf's article, "Medals," Jewish Encyclopedia, Vol. VIII, 1907, but this may be a misprint)*

> Hungarian National Museum, Budapest (43 or 44 mm; silver)
> Hungarian National Museum, Budapest (41 mm; both bronze and tin)
> American Numismatic Society, N.Y.C. (41 mm; silver)
> Collection of B. Kirschner, Jerusalem

1686   Same, with slight variations, main one being that the inscription on reverse extends an additional line.

> *38 and 42 mm; silver and bronze; MB (Monogram of Martin Brunner)*

> Budapest National Museum, Budapest (38 mm; bronze)
> Schimko Collection, Hungary No. 74, O. Gohl, *Budapest emlékérmei,* 1899 (42 mm; silver)

1687   The Pharisee Risen from Death. German. Obverse, a Jew swathed in prayer shawl; reverse, a Negro dwarf swallowing a camel while reaching for gnats that swarm on flowers nearby. Reference to Matt. 23:24: "Ye blind guides, which strain at a gnat and swallow a camel." On rim, the letters "CFP"; that is, "With Frederick's Permission."

> *42 and 44 x 45 mm; silver; Christian Wermuth*

> State Museum of Berlin
> Listed in Domanig's *Die deutsche Medaille . . .* (44 x 45 mm) No. 840
> Listed in M. J. Meissner's *Ueber Christian Wermuth und seine satyrischen Medaillen* No. 14
> Illustrated in Bernhart's *Medaillen und Plaketten* (42 mm), p. 77

1694   "Korn Jude." Jew carrying a sack of grain. German. Obverse, Jew faces right and bears a sack on which a perched devil is opening the mouth (i.e., taking his share); reverse, on upright grain sifter (called in various descriptions a ring, a wheel or a bushel measure) a quotation from Proverbs 11:26 stating that those who withhold corn are cursed by the people. Reference is to grain speculation causing famine or an "expensive time." Jews were often accused of this practice. Considered to have been issued in Silesia.

> *36 mm; silver and lead; by Christian Wermuth, according to Meissner*

> The Jewish Museum, N.Y.C. (silver)
> The Kadman Numismatic Museum, Tel Aviv (silver)
> Collection of Arthur Polak, Amsterdam (silver)
> Collection of Bruno Kisch, N.Y.C. (two silver and lead)

Collection of Author, N.Y.C. (silver)

Collection of Alfred Rubens, London (silver); this piece is misdated as 1624

Listed in Brettauer's *Medicina in Nummis* No. 1900

Listed in Pfeiffer and Ruland's *Pestilentia in Nummis* No. 75

1694   "Korn Jude." Similar to above, but Jew on obverse faces left.

36 mm; tin, lead, and bronze

Listed in auction catalog of C. Fieweger, Berlin, 1885 Nos. 82, 83, and 84

1694   "Korn Jude." Similar. Jew on obverse faces right, but grain sifter on reverse is horizontal.

34 and 41 mm; bronze, silver, tin, and lead

The Jewish Museum, N.Y.C. (34 mm; silver)

Collection of Bruno Kisch, N.Y.C. (34 mm; silver)

Listed in Pfeiffer and Ruland's *Pestilentia in Nummis* (34 mm; silver) No. 76

Ibid. (34 mm; tin) No. 77

Listed in auction catalog of C. Fieweger, Berlin, 1885 (41mm; lead) No. 80

Listed in M. J. Meissner's *Ueber Christian Wermuth und seine satyrischen Medaillen* No. 1

1694   "Korn Jude." Similar. Jew on obverse faces left and grain sifter on reverse is horizontal. Some stated as issued in Silesia while others are claimed to be from Hamburg.

34 and 41 or 42 mm; silver, pewter, and silver-plated copper

National Museum, Jerusalem (41 or 42 mm; pewter)

The Kadman Numismatic Museum, Tel Aviv (41 or 42 mm; silver)

Listed in auction catalog of C. Fieweger, Berlin, 1885 (34 mm; silver-plated copper) No. 81

Listed in Brettauer's *Medicina in Nummis* (41 mm; silver) No. 1899

1695   "Korn Jude." Obverse, house of peasant, barn, and farmland, with Jew hanging from tree and devil securing rope. Reference to Luke 12, attacking covetousness. Reverse, same quotation from

Proverbs, with grain sifter horizontal. Issued in Silesia, Germany. Some have quotation from Proverbs on inside and outside of horizontal grain sifter; others only on the outside. "Easy time"; i.e., the famine period has ended.

32 and 34 mm; silver and copper; by Christian Wermuth, according to Meissner

Collection of Arthur Polak, Amsterdam (34 mm; silver; 32 mm; copper)

Listed in Pfeiffer and Ruland's *Pestilentia in Nummis* (34 mm; silver) No. 78

Listed in M. J. Meissner's *Ueber Christian Wermuth und seine satyrischen Medaillen* No. 2

Listed in Brettauer's *Medicina in Nummis* (34 mm; silver and copper) No. 1902

1695   "Korn Jude." Obverse, same as above; reverse, Jew faces right carrying a sack of grain in typical type.

34 mm; silver; Christian Wermuth

Listed in Pfeiffer and Ruland's *Pestilentia in Nummis* No. 79

1696   "Korn Jude." Same as 1694. Jew on obverse faces right and the grain sifter on reverse is vertical. "Expensive time"; i.e., again a famine year.

36 mm; tin

Hebrew Union College Museum, Cincinnati

ca. 1700   "Feder Jude." Jew with feathers in cap and sack on back. Obverse, Jew facing left and carrying large sack on back and a small sack or money bag in hand; reverse and continued on rim, pejorative inscription implying Jews pimp for the rulers and the cuckolded husbands are rewarded by public office. Inscription is mixed German and Latin. Reference to feathers seems to be used in the same sense as horns in cuckolding. Most Feder Judes state "I wear the feathers . . ."; but some state instead "I wear the horns. . . ." Small variations also occur in the reverse inscription.

42 and 43 mm; silver, pewter, and bronze; C.W. (i.e., Christian Wermuth); not dated

The Jewish Museum, N.Y.C. (silver)
Hebrew Union College Museum, Cincinnati (pewter)
National Museum, Jerusalem (pewter)
Collection of Arthur Polak, Amsterdam (bronze)
Listed in M. J. Meissner's *Ueber Christian Wermuth und seine satyrischen Medaillen* No. 12.
Listed in *Blätter für Münzfreunde* No. 76, Col. 644 (silver)

ca. 1700   "Feder Jude." The same but Jew facing right.

42 and 43 mm; pewter; not dated

Listed in the auction catalog of C. Fieweger, Berlin, 1885, Nos. 77 and 78

ca. 1700   "Feder Jude." The same but on the large sack of the Jew is inscribed "The Trial."

42 mm; thick pewter; not dated

Listed in the auction catalog of C. Fieweger, Berlin, 1885, No. 79

ca. 1700   "Feder Jude." Obverse, the same but without "The Trial" and Jew facing left; reverse, dragon tamed by two cupids with legend "Amor Vincit Omnia."

41 to 44 mm; silver, pewter, and tin; probably by Wermuth; not dated

The Jewish Museum, N.Y.C. (41 mm; pewter)
Listed in auction catalog of C. Fieweger, Berlin, 1885 (42 mm; silver) No. 77. Also (43 mm; tin) No. 78
44-mm size mentioned by Kirschner in *Deutsche Spottmedaillen auf Juden*, item No. 12

ca. 1700   "Feder Jude." Obverse, the same and Jew facing left but without legends; reverse, lion tamed by cupid with legend "Amor Vincit Omnia."

47 x 42, 46 x 42 and 45 x 40 mm (ovals); silver; probably by Wermuth; not dated

State Museum of Berlin
Listed in Brettauer's *Medicina in Nummis* (46 x 42) No. 4765

Listed in Domanig's *Die deutsche Medaille* . . . (46 x 42)
No. 839

Listed in *Münzen und Medaillen*, Basel, List 56 (45 x 40)
No. 112

Listed in auction catalog of Karl Kress, Munich, 107th auction
(47 x 42) No. 1631. Kress states the piece was issued in
Hamburg by a medalist named Johann Reteke.

ca. 1700   False Integrity of Jews, Bad Priests, and Tricky Lawyers. Obverse,
a wolf and fox, Latin captions overhead; reverse, pejorative inscription in German. Supposedly refers to a priest named F. J.
Mayer.

> *41 mm; silver; thought to be by Christian Wermuth; not
> dated*

Collection of Bruno Kisch, N.Y.C.

Listed in Meissner's *Ueber Christian Wermuth und seine
satyrischen Medaillen* No. 15

Listed in Gaedechens' *Hamburgische Münzen und Medaillen*,
Vol. II, p. 22, No. 12

Listed in auction catalog of Karl Kress, Munich, 115th auction, No. 5616

ca. 1700   Same, but obverse shows a pack of wolves hunting in a landscape
and the reverse inscription has Old German spelling.

> *silver; probably by Christian Wermuth; not dated*

Sole listing in Moritz Stern's *Aus dem Berliner Jüdischen
Museum*. Without verification, Kirschner claims it to be
44 mm.

ca. 1700   The Useless Baptism of Jews. German. Obverse, Jew baptized to
avoid being drowned, with millstone around neck; reverse, pejorative inscription.

> *42 to 44 mm; silver and silvered bronze; by Christian
> Wermuth, according to Meissner; not dated*

The Jewish Museum, N.Y.C.
Hebrew Union College Museum, Cincinnati
National Museum, Jerusalem
Collection of Arthur Polak, Amsterdam

Collection of Bruno Kisch, N.Y.C. (two examples)

Listed in M. J. Meissner's *Ueber Christian Wermuth und seine satyrischen Medaillen* No. 13

1711   Fire in the Frankfurt am Main Jewish Ghetto. German. Obverse, the fire before which stand a family of four Jews, with hands stretched up in lament; reverse, inscription in Latin describing "happy day" when ghetto burned but Christian buildings nearby were not affected. Date established by chronogram.

> *Three variations:*
> a. *44 mm; silver; C.W. (i.e., Christian Wermuth)*
> b. *44 mm; tin. Lacks initials and writing is smaller than on silver type; rim inscription is missing*
> c. *44 mm; lead; lacks initials and a slight change in the Latin of last lines*

The Jewish Museum, N.Y.C. (a)*

Historical Museum of Frankfurt am Main (a)

Collection of Arthur Polak, Amsterdam (a)

Hebrew Union College Museum, Cincinnati (a and b)

State Museum of Berlin

Collection of Bruno Kisch, N.Y.C. (a)

Collection of Author, N.Y.C. (a)*

Last variant (c) reported in *Die Munzen von Frankfurt am Main* by Fellner and Joseph—former Rommich Collection, Germany

Listed in Kirschner's *Deutsche Spottmedaillen auf Juden* No. 33, as also being struck in bronze

1711   Fire in the Frankfurt am Main Jewish Ghetto. Obverse, view of city of Frankfurt with eagle overhead; reverse, inscription in German cast in verse form stating the facts of the fire without mockery.

> *50 mm; silver; Johann Linck*

Hebrew Union College Museum, Cincinnati

Historical Museum, Frankfurt am Main

* Both examples of the dominant type that the writer has examined with great care indicate die defects to the right on the obverse. It may be that late strikings were made from the obsolete dies.

1721   The Four Big Frankfurt am Main Fires in the Last Decade. Obverse, view of Frankfurt with burning houses, and eagle overhead; reverse, inscription in German cursing Jews for not becoming Christians. Date established by chronogram.

45 mm; silver and tin; C.W. (i.e., Christian Wermuth)

Hebrew Union College Museum, Cincinnati (tin)
National Museum, Jerusalem (tin)
Listed in Kirschner's *Deutsche Spottmedaillen auf Juden* No. 35, as also being struck in bronze and copper

1728   Conversion of Jews and Moslems to Christ. German. Obverse, sailing boat with mast in the form of a cross and legend, "The Waters Stood Still in Amazement"; reverse, inscription commemorating the beginning of a serious effort to convert Jews and Mohammedans to Christ.

25 mm; tin; C.W. (i.e., Christian Wermuth)

The Jewish Museum, N.Y.C.
Listed in *Blätter für Münzfreunde*, 1907, p. 3765

1728   Same as above but obverse legend is "In the Evening There Will be Light" and initials of medalist are not on the side of the sailing boat.

25 mm; tin

Listed in the Wellenheim Catalog, Vienna, 1845, II, 2, No. 15409

1738   Hanging of "Jud Joseph Süs," Joseph Suskind Oppenheimer, at Stuttgart. German. Obverse, bust to left, with wig; reverse, gallows and pejorative legend. "Jud Süs" was the much-hated financial minister to the Duke of Württemberg.

33, 36, 37, 38, and 40 mm; white metal or pewter, lead, and bronze

The Jewish Museum, N.Y.C. (37 mm; lead)
Hebrew Union College Museum, Cincinnati (36 mm; lead)
Collection of Arthur Polak, Amsterdam (40 mm; lead)
State Coin Collection of Munich (33 mm; bronze)
County Museum of Baden, Karlsruhe

Collection of Alfred Rubens, London (38 mm; white metal)
National Museum, Jerusalem (38 mm; lead)
Collection of Bruno Kisch, N.Y.C. (38 mm; pewter; also
    36 mm; bronze)

1738   Same except on obverse there is a spray of flowers to the left of the
        bust; and on reverse a bird is flying toward the caged victim with
        a letter in its mouth. Obvious allusion to the notorious gallantry
        of "Jud Süs" with the ladies.

        37.5 mm; lead

        The Jewish Museum, N.Y.C.
        The Kadman Numismatic Museum, Tel Aviv

1738   Variant of above. Obverse, bust to left; reverse, top part shows
        Jud Joseph Süs trying to escape in carriage while, below, cart is
        being pulled toward gallows from which a man is dangling.

        32, 37, and 40 mm; silver, tin, and lead

        Collection of Arthur Polak, Amsterdam (40 mm; silver)
        State Coin Collection of Munich (32 mm; tin)
        Collection of Bruno Kisch, N.Y.C. (37 mm; lead)

1738   Variant again. Obverse, bust to right with beard and halter round
        neck; reverse, gallows with different pejorative legend. Also
        added, "in Stuttgard Executed Feb. 4, 1738."

        31 mm; lead

        The Jewish Museum, N.Y.C.

1738*   "Schraub" or Screw-Medal of Jud Joseph Süs. Obverse and re-
        verse of medal, showing bust and gallows, separated and the two
        sides fitted to screw together to make a case. Inside, 19 pictures,
        hand painted on parchment or copper plates, showing his life and
        death.

        41.5 mm; silver

        The Jewish Museum of Prague
        State Coin Collection of Munich

        * Some of these screw medals may have been made in later years.

Mint Cabinet of Stuttgart (inside pictures missing)
National Museum, Jerusalem
Collection of F. Sternberg, Zurich

1738*   "Schraub" or Screw-Medal of Jud Joseph Süs, but obverse shows
bust and reverse Süs trying to escape in carriage while, below, cart
is pulled toward gallows.

42 mm; silver

State Museum of Berlin

1770–   "Korn Jude." Dated 1770 on obverse and 1771 on reverse. Ob-
1771   verse, a fat Jew walking toward open jaws of an alligator and
facing left with staff and grain sack in which a devil is opening
the mouth; reverse, listing of food prices.

29 mm; silvered brass; Io. Ch. Reich-Fürth (Bavaria)

Collection of Bruno Kisch, N.Y.C. (two examples)

1771–   "Korn Jude." Same as 1770–1771 except dated 1772 on obverse
1772   and 1771 on reverse. Jew faces left.

*29 or 30 mm; brass and copper; Io. Ch. Reich-Fürth
(Bavaria)*

The Jewish Museum, N.Y.C. (brass)
Collection of Arthur Polak, Amsterdam (copper)
Listed in Pfeiffer and Ruland's *Pestilentia in Nummis* No. 135
Listed in Brettauer's *Medicina in Nummis* No. 1909

1771–   "Korn Jude." Dated 1772 on obverse and 1771 on reverse. Ob-
1772   verse, Jew facing left, usual depiction of 1694 except a goat,
rather than a devil, is on the sack; reverse, listing of food prices
(i.e., showing inflation of prices). On rim, inscription telling
Jews to go to the devil.

29 mm; pewter; Io. Ch. Reich-Fürth (Bavaria)

Listed in L. Pfeiffer's *Pestilentia in Nummis* No. 30

(Note: The devil is shown crouched forward with extended legs.
When the coin is worn, the figure might be mistaken for a goat,
as Pfeiffer lists it.)

* Idem.

1771– "Korn Jude." Dated 1771–1772 on obverse. Obverse, Jew facing
1772 right with sack of grain over shoulders on which a devil sits,
belling him, while a woman implores aid; reverse, same quotation
from Proverbs as earlier medals, grain sifter upright. Issued in
Thuringia, Germany.

39 mm; lead

The Jewish Museum, N.Y.C.
The Kadman Numismatic Museum, Tel Aviv
Collection of Bruno Kisch, N.Y.C. (two examples)

1771– "Korn Jude." Dated 1772 on obverse and 1771 on reverse. Ob-
1772 verse, fat Jew walking toward open jaws of an alligator and facing
left with staff and grain sack in which a devil is opening the mouth;
reverse, listing of food prices. Issued in Fürth, Bavaria.

29 or 30 mm; brass and copper; Reich

The Jewish Museum, N.Y.C. (brass)
Collection of Arthur Polak, Amsterdam (copper)

1771– "Korn Jude." Same as above, but Jew faces right.
1772
      29 mm; brass and lead; Io. Ch. Reich-Fürth (Bavaria)

Listed in auction catalog of C. Fieweger, Berlin, 1885 (brass)
No. 88
Listed in Pfeiffer and Ruland's *Pestilentia in Nummis* (lead)
No. 136

1624– "Korn Jude." Same as 1694. Underneath date is 1624–1772.
1772
      35 to 37 mm; silver, tin, and lead

Woburn House Jewish Museum, London (35 mm; silver)
Collection of B. Kirschner, Jerusalem (37 mm; tin; Jew faces
right)
Listed in Pfeiffer and Ruland's *Pestilentia in Nummis* (36 mm;
lead) No. 129

(Note: The writer feels that these medals have been misdated and
should read 1694–1772.)

1772 "Korn Jude." Same as 1694. Jew facing right, grain sifter upright.
      38 or 39 mm; lead

The Jewish Museum, N.Y.C.

Woburn House Jewish Museum, London
Listed in Pfeiffer and Ruland's *Pestilentia in Nummis* No. 127
Ibid., but medal has letters "C.G.R.U." No. 128

1772 "Korn Jude." Same as 1694. Jew facing right, grain sifter horizontal.

30 mm; tin or pewter

Collection of Arthur Polak, Amsterdam

1694– "Korn Jude." Same as 1694 except Jew in landscape, facing
1772 right, is shown as very fat and underneath date is 1694–1772.
Grain sifter is upright. Issued in Thuringia, Germany.

39 mm; lead, tin, and pewter; "C.G.R.U."

The Jewish Museum, N.Y.C. (pewter)
Collection of Bruno Kisch, N.Y.C. (lead)
Listed in Brettauer's *Medicina in Nummis* (tin) No. 1904

1694– "Korn Jude." Obverse, Jew facing right, devil opening mouth of
1772 sack, while a woman implores aid. Dated March 12, and then
1694–1772. Reverse, same quotation from Proverbs, grain sifter
upright. Issued in Thuringia, Germany.

39 mm; pewter; some "C.G.R.U."

Collection of Bruno Kisch, N.Y.C. (no "C.G.R.U." shown)
Listed in L. Pfeiffer's *Pestilentia in Nummis* No. 29
Listed in Pfeiffer and Ruland's *Pestilentia in Nummis* No. 130
Listed in Brettauer's *Medicina in Nummis* No. 1905

1694– "Korn Jude." Same as above but Jew facing left.
1772
39 mm; lead

Listed in auction catalog of C. Fieweger, Berlin, 1885, No. 85

1694– "Korn Jude." Same as above but all lettering is smaller and in
1772 script.

39 mm; lead

Listed in auction catalog of C. Fieweger, Berlin, 1885, No. 86

1772 "Korn Jude." Obverse, fat Jew walking toward open jaws of an
alligator and facing left with staff and grain sack in which a devil

is opening the mouth; reverse, usual quotation from Proverbs, grain sifter horizontal.

29 or 30 mm; silver, tin, and lead; Reich

The Jewish Museum, N.Y.C. (silver)
Hebrew Union College Museum, Cincinnati (tin)
Listed in Pfeiffer and Ruland's *Pestilentia in Nummis* No. 134

1772   "Korn Jude." Obverse, same but Jew facing right; reverse grain sifter horizontal with legend above, "Fear God."

24 and 30 or 31 mm; tin or pewter; Io. Ch. Reich

Collection of Abraham E. Millgram, Jerusalem (pewter)
Listed in Brettauer's *Medicina in Nummis* (30 or 31 mm; tin or pewter) No. 1908
Listed in Pfeiffer and Ruland's *Pestilentia in Nummis* (30 or 31 mm; tin or pewter) No. 137
Listed in auction catalog of C. Fieweger, Berlin, 1885 (24 mm; tin) No. 89

1772   "Korn Jude." Obverse, same but Jew facing left; reverse, same as above.

29 or 30 mm; tin or pewter; Io. Ch. Reich

Collection of B. Kirschner, Jerusalem
Listed in Brettauer's *Medicina in Nummis* No. 1910
Listed in Pfeiffer and Ruland's *Pestilentia in Nummis* No. 133

1772   "Korn Jude." Obverse, corn harvest and haystack with bushel containing 15 ears of corn and legend, "We want this fertility"; reverse, Jew hanging in a barn and legend, "But I did hope for famine time." Issued in Thuringia, Germany. Apparently autumn harvest was excellent, and speculators were ruined.

40 and 43 mm; tin or pewter and lead

Listed in Brettauer's *Medicina in Nummis* (40 mm; tin or pewter) No. 1907
Listed in Pfeiffer and Ruland's *Pestilentia in Nummis* (40 mm; tin or pewter) No. 131
Listed in auction catalog of C. Fieweger, Berlin, 1885 (43 mm; lead) No. 87

1665–   "Korn Jude." Dated 1665–1773. (No more information.)
1773   Listed in unpublished material of the late Dr. Bruno Kirschner.
        This is not reported elsewhere and may be apocryphal.

1772–   Dated 1772 on obverse and 1773 on reverse. Obverse, woman ap-
1773   pealing to richly dressed Jew, facing left, with sacks of grain
        stacked behind him; reverse, same man hung from tree and legend
        stating that avarice is the root of all evil.

> *38 mm; pewter or tin*

> The Jewish Museum, N.Y.C.
> Listed in Pfeiffer and Ruland's *Pestilentia in Nummis* No. 132

1809   "Shylock." English. Obverse, bust of Jew and legend: "This is
        the Jew, which Shakespeare drew"; reverse, a garland of oak and
        initials. Related to the Covent Garden Theatre riots in 1809, where
        Jews acted as "strike breakers" to support the position of manage-
        ment on higher prices.

> *38 and 44 mm; white metal and bronze; V.P. (i.e., Vox Pop-*
> *uli); not dated*

> The Jewish Museum, N.Y.C. (38 mm; white metal)
> Collection of Abraham E. Millgram, Jerusalem (44 mm;
>   bronze)

2. *Marranos and Christian Converts*

1518   Portrait of Antonio Gonzalo de Toledo, physician in Lyons,
        France. Obverse, "ANTHONIVS. DE. TOLEDO. MEDICINE.
        DOCTOR—1518," with bust to right with a large cap; reverse,
        "NON. TOLEDI. TABVLA. EST. ISTA. SED. EST. SPECVLVM"
        with nude woman seated on a saddle, a basket of fruits on her
        head, and holding a vase of flowers in one hand and plants in the
        other. The date may also be read as 1515.

> *47 or 48 mm; bronze; possibly by Jeronyme Henry*

> Mazerolle 43
> Dreyfus 532
> Armand II, 137, 11 Anon.
> National Gallery of Art, Washington, D.C.
> Fillon Collection (mentioned in Mazerolle)

1555   Portrait of Ursula Lópes at time of Marriage to Marcus Pérez.
        Flemish couple of Spanish origin, apparently struck in Italy. Ob-
        verse, "VRSVLAE. LOPES. M.P.C. AET. XVIII.—1555," with
        bust to left and veil falling to rear; no reverse. An aunt of Michel
        de Montaigne, Ursula Lópes was the daughter of Martin Lópes
        de Villanova. Husband and wife became ardent Calvinists though
        of Marrano origin.

   64 mm; bronze; Pastorino de' Pastorini

   Armand III, 86, P
   Formerly in Otto Goldschmidt Collection of Gotha, Germany.
       Medal was not included when the collection was retrieved
       after World War II
   Formerly listed in the Collection Vasset, Paris

1580   Portrait of Ursula Lópes Pérez. Flemish. Marcus Pérez, her hus-
        band, died in 1572 at the age of forty-five. His widow returned to
        Antwerp, her native city, in 1579, with her twelve children. Medal
        was struck one year later, when Ursula was forty-three. She died
        the same year.

   Listed on page 584 of *Étude sur les Colonies marchandes
       méridionales à Anvers de 1488 à 1567,* by Jan Albert Goris

1597   Portrait of Luis Pérez for his sixty-sixth birthday in Antwerp. Ob-
        verse, "LVDOVICVS. PEREZ. AET. LXVI," with bust to right
        and long moustache; reverse, "IN X̄PO VITA—1597." Luis Pérez
        was a brother of Marcus Pérez and, though of Marrano origin, be-
        came a Calvinist preacher.

   37 mm; silver and bronze; probably by Jakob Jonghelink

   Armand III, 310, F, Anon.
   Royal Coin Cabinet, The Hague
   Cabinet national de France, Paris

1659   Jew Michael of Prague and his Baptism in Nürnberg. Obverse,
        coats-of-arms of Nürnberg overhead and the baptism of Jesus in
        the Jordan; reverse, coats-of-arms of Michael's three patrician
        godfathers and inscription relating to his baptism and new name
        of Burckhardt Christoph Leonhard.

   82 x 69 mm in oval; cast silver

Listed in Christoph Andreas, Dem Viertem, Im Hof. *Sammlung eines Nürnbergischen Münz-Cabinets* (Vol. 2), p. 108, Nürnberg, 1782.

18th-century coppered lead copy in collection of Herbert J. Erlanger, N.Y.C.

1714　　The Baptism of Crainfeld in Heidelberg, Germany. Obverse, figure and flaming altar; reverse, inscription in Latin with name of godfather. Example of "patenpfennig" or godfather penny.

51 mm; silver; D.P.

County Museum of Heidelberg

1752　　Memorial on the death of Hermann Bartholomaeus Hoedemaker, convert to Christianity. Obverse, coffin and funeral urn, with figure and palm tree; reverse, inscription in Dutch stating he was "an Israelite in whom there was no guile."

85 x 70; oval; embossed silver

Collection of Arthur Polak, Amsterdam

1797　　Commemoration of Franz Anton von Sonnenfels for founding a school for the poor in Nikolsburg, Moravia. Obverse, woman and children at altar; reverse, inscription to von Sonnenfels. Franz and his brother Joseph, the famous writer, were both baptized in early youth.

41 x 38 with loop; oval; silver; I. Donner

The Jewish Museum, N.Y.C.

Late
18th
Century
Antonius Raphael Mengs, German Painter. Obverse, portrait; reverse, desk with book, lyre, and palette on top and legend "Pictor Philosophus"

39 mm

Reproduced on the title page of *The Works of Anthony Raphael Mengs*, translated by Joseph Nicholas D'Azara. London, 1796

3. *The Slow Rise of Jewish Emancipation*

1745   Repeal of Edict Expelling Jews from Prague. Obverse, audience before Maria Theresa; reverse, burning of object at court (or, as usually assumed, thanksgiving offered at the Temple of Jerusalem). Tremendous pressure was put on the Austrian court through the Jewish communities of England and Holland to cancel the expulsion decree. This medal was issued by the Dutch Jews.

> *64 mm; silver and pewter; N.V.S.F. (Nicholaas van Swinderen F.)*

> The Jewish Museum, N.Y.C. (silver)
> Royal Coin Cabinet, The Hague (silver)
> Collection of Arthur Polak, Amsterdam (silver and pewter)
> American Numismatic Society, N.Y.C. (silver)

ca. 1777   Homage of the Darmstadt Jews on the Occasion of the birth of the Great Duke Ludwig II of Hesse. The rulers of Hesse and Darmstadt were unusually tolerant in this period.

> *33 mm; gold; not dated*

> Formerly in the Otto Goldschmidt Collection of Gotha, Germany. Medal was not included when the collection was retrieved after World War II. This medal is not recorded elsewhere and the date is only established by the facts stated.

1781   Edict of Toleration of Austrian Emperor Joseph II, son of Maria Theresa. Obverse, bust; reverse, memorial with standing figure. Religious liberty granted in Austrian territory to Protestants and Jews. Joseph II was a benevolent despot who tried to liberalize Austrian rule. The edict became a dead letter after the Emperor died.

> *45 mm; silver and pewter; OE. (i.e., Oexlein)*

> The Jewish Museum, N.Y.C. (two examples in pewter)
> Woburn House Jewish Museum, London (listed as white metal)
> National Museum, Jerusalem (silver and pewter)
> Collection of Arthur Polak, Amsterdam (pewter)
> The Kadman Numismatic Museum, Tel Aviv (silver)
> Collection of Bruno Kisch, N.Y.C. (pewter)

American Numismatic Society, N.Y.C. (silver)

Collection of Author, N.Y.C. (pewter)

1782   Edict of Toleration of Austrian Emperor Joseph II. Obverse, similar-type bust as 1781; reverse, three figures, each representing one of the three religions in the Empire. Some have the last words of obverse legend, "Tolerantia Imperantis" on open scroll; others do not and the letters are larger.

    silver and pewter; Reich

    40 mm

Collection of Bruno Kisch, N.Y.C. (pewter)

    43 to 45 mm

The Jewish Museum, N.Y.C. (43 mm; silver; not on scroll. Also 43.5 mm; pewter; not on scroll)

Hebrew Union College Museum, Cincinnati (43 mm; silver; on scroll. Also 43 mm; pewter; on scroll)

National Museum, Jerusalem (43.5 mm; silver; not on scroll. Also 43.5 mm; pewter; on scroll)

Museum of Jewish Art, Paris (45 mm; silver; on scroll)

The Kadman Numismatic Museum, Tel Aviv (43.5 mm; silver; not on scroll)

American Numismatic Society, N.Y.C. (43 mm; silver; on scroll. Also 43 mm; silver; not on scroll. Also 45 mm; pewter; on scroll)

Collection of Rabbi Abraham E. Millgram, Jerusalem (43 mm; silver; on scroll)

Collection of Bruno Kisch, N.Y.C. (43 mm; silver. Also 43 mm; pewter)

Collection of Author, N.Y.C. (43 mm; silver; not on scroll)

Woburn House Jewish Museum, London (45 mm; listed as white metal; on scroll)

Collection of Arthur Polak, Amsterdam (43 mm; silver; on scroll)

The Jewish Museum, Budapest (43 mm; pewter; not on scroll)

1782   Same as above but on obverse Latin legend "Imp." (for "Imperator") is spelled out and the final words "Tolerantia Imperantis" are excluded.

    45 and 47 mm; pewter; R (i.e., Reich)

Royal Coin Cabinet, The Hague (45 mm)
Collection of Arthur Polak, Amsterdam (47 mm)
National Museum, Jerusalem (47 mm; two copies)

1782   Same as above but reverse shows a kneeling figure next to an altar.

44 mm; pewter

Collection of Bruno Kisch, N.Y.C.

1790   Homage to Landgrave Ludwig X of Hesse and Darmstadt (later
        Great Duke Ludwig I). Obverse, woman sacrificing; reverse, in-
        scription in Latin. Presentation by Hessian Jews in gratitude for
        religious liberty.

37 mm; silver; H.B. (i.e., Johann Heinrich Boltschauser)

National Museum, Jerusalem
Darmstadt, Hesse Land Museum
Listed in J. Hoffmeister's *Hessische Münzen*, Vol. II, No. 4029

1790   Homage to Landgravine Louise Caroline Henriette of Hesse and
        Darmstadt. Obverse, palm tree and legend; reverse, inscription.
        Presentation in gratitude for her aid in the fight for religious
        liberty. Two variants: some have a period, others not, after the ob-
        verse legend.

34 mm; silver

The Jewish Museum, N.Y.C. (no period)
Listed in J. Hoffmeister's *Hessische Münzen*, Vol. II, No. 4030

1790   Same as above except smaller, the obverse legend is in a double
        line and the palm tree has heavier fronds.

29 mm; silver

The Jewish Museum, N.Y.C.
Collection of Arthur Polak, Amsterdam
Listed in J. Hoffmeister's *Hessische Münzen*, Vol. II, No. 4031

1796   Commemoration of Equal Rights Granted Jews in Batavian Re-
        public, i.e., Holland under the French. Obverse, leafy twigs
        grouped around emblem surmounted by hat; reverse, inscription
        in Dutch. Many Dutch Jews were enthusiastic partisans of the
        French Revolution.

36 mm; copper

Royal Coin Cabinet, The Hague

1805   Czar Alexander I of Russia Frees the Jews from a Special Tax (not from compulsory life in the Pale). Obverse, bust; reverse, man praying before altar with flame. Alexander I went through an early liberal phase before he returned to reactionary policies.

> *46 mm; silver; P.M. (i.e., Paul Merker); a unique copy in gold was also struck for the Czar*

The Jewish Museum, N.Y.C.
Collection of Alfred Rubens, London
County Museum of Baden, Karlsruhe
The Kadman Numismatic Museum, Tel Aviv

1806   Sanhedrin of Napoleon. Obverse, bust of Napoleon; reverse, Napoleon and Moses. Religious freedom and state protection were given to the Jews by Napoleon in return for which the rabbis ruled that Jewish soldiers were freed from religious obligations during military service. The medal most amusingly depicts Moses bowing to the Emperor.

> *41 mm; silver, lead, and bronze; DePaulis on obverse and Dupres on reverse; also marked Directeur Denon (of the French Mint) on obverse*

This medal is very common. Restrikes are available at La Médaille, 11 Quai de Conti, Paris VI, France.

1808   Enfranchisement of the Jews of Westphalia. Obverse, woman in prayer before altar on which rest Tables of Law; reverse, two winged figures. The decree was issued by Jerome Bonaparte and revoked by the native Germans after the fall of Napoleon.

> *42.5 mm; silver and bronze; Abramson*

The Jewish Museum, N.Y.C. (silver)
National Museum, Jerusalem (silver and bronze)
Collection of Arthur Polak, Amsterdam (bronze)
State Art Collections of Cassel (silver)
City Museum of Brunswick (silver and bronze)
Collection of Alfred Rubens, London (silver)

4. *Medals Commemorating Individual Jews*

1552 Portraits of Elia Delatas and his Mother, Rica Delatas. Italian. Obverse, "ELIA. DELATAS. EBREO. MD52" with bust to right with beard; reverse, "RICA. SVA. GIENETRICE." with bust to right. Elia Delatas was the son of Emanuele Lattes, physician, and grandson of Bonet de Lattes, famous physician and astronomer.

> *38, 39, or 40 mm; cast bronze (Also listed in Albert Wolf's article, "Medals," Jewish Encyclopedia, Vol. VIII, 1907, as 49 mm—this may be a misprint.)*

Armand II, 231, 10, Anon.
The Jewish Museum, N.Y.C.
Collection of Alfred Rubens, London
Formerly listed in the Spitzer Collection, Paris

1557 Portrait of Abramo Emanuele Norsa (or Norcia). Italian. Obverse, "ABR. EMA. NVR—1557" with bust to right with long beard; no reverse. Abramo Norsa was a banker and Jewish communal leader of Ferrara, Italy. The Norsas were a powerful Italian Jewish family for many generations.

> *41 mm; cast bronze; Pastorino de' Pastorini*

Armand III, 87, U
Formerly in the Royal Cabinet Museum of Parma, now part of the Pilotta Museum of Parma. The medal was stolen during World War II.

1558 Portrait of Gratzia Nasi. Cast in Italy. Obverse, name in Hebrew letters to left top and "A.AE. XVIII" to right top with bust to left; no reverse. Date has also been stated as 1557 as well. Gratzia (Gracia) Nasi was married to the brother of Don Joseph Nasi, Duke of Naxos, and was niece of the well-known Marrano heiress, Gracia Nasi (1510–1568). This is the first unequivocal Jewish medal with a Hebrew legend.

> *66 mm; cast bronze; Pastorino de' Pastorini*

Armand I, 202, 86
The Jewish Museum, N.Y.C.

Hebrew Union College Museum, Cincinnati
National Museum, Jerusalem
Cabinet national de France, Paris
Collection of Author, N.Y.C.
Collection of Sigmund Harrison, Ardmore, Pa.
Collection of the late Herman Davidowitz, N.Y.C.

1667   Presentation to Josef Athias by the Dutch States-General for publishing the "Athias Bible." This Bible, in Hebrew, achieved an international reputation.

   gold

   Listed in Arthur Polak's *Joodse Penningen in de Nederlanden.* Reportedly only one lost example.

1673   Elias Lindo, Broker's Medal, London. Pendent type. Obverse, the Royal Arms; reverse, arms of City of London with space beneath for name of broker. This is a predecessor to the "Jew Brokers' medals." In 1697, twelve Jews were allowed to be brokers on the Royal Exchange in London. The Lindo family preserved these medals.

   39 mm; silver

   Guildhall Museum, London

1697   Elias Lindo. Same as 1673. "Jew Broker" under the new arrangement.

   Guildhall Museum, London

1714   Silver wedding of Jacob and Hanna Bassan, Holland. 3rd Sivan 5475. Obverse, child and palm tree with harbor background; reverse, inscription in Dutch framed in curtains. Nothing more is known of this Dutch couple.

   80 mm; bronze

   Collection of Arthur Polak, Amsterdam

1722   Dr. Abraham Gomes de Sylva in Amsterdam. Commemorating his entry into the Amsterdam Medical Society. Not included in Arthur Polak's book.

   bronze

Listed in Moritz Stern's *Aus dem Berliner Jüdischen Museum.*
This collection disappeared under the Nazis.

1728   Isaac Lindo, Jr. Not pendent type but otherwise the same as 1673.
"Jew Broker."

Guildhall Museum, London

1735   Eleazar ben Samuel Shmelka, Chief Rabbi of Brody. Obverse,
bust; reverse, inscription according welcome by Ashkenazi community at Amsterdam on his appointment as rabbi. Rabbi Eleazar
eventually moved to Palestine, where he died in 1741.

*45 and 48 mm; silver, copper, and lead; Joel, son of Rabbi
Lippman Levi (initials on reverse)*

The Jewish Museum, N.Y.C. (48 mm; copper)
Hebrew Union College Museum, Cincinnati (48 mm; silver
and lead)
Jewish Historical Museum, Amsterdam (48 mm; silvered
copper)
National Museum, Jerusalem (48 mm; lead, silver alloy)
Collection of Arthur Polak, Amsterdam (48 mm; silver)
Collection of Alfred Rubens, London (45 mm; silver)

1749   Golden Anniversary of Benjamin and Rachel Henriques. Nothing
more is known outside of this description. Probably Dutch, but
not mentioned in Arthur Polak's book.

32 mm; gold

Formerly in Otto Goldschmidt Collection of Gotha, Germany.
Medal was not included when the collection was retrieved
after World War II.

1763   Elias Lindo. Same as 1728. "Jew Broker."

Guildhall Museum, London

ca. 1770   Veitel-Heine Ephraim. Obverse, king caressing cheeks of Ephraim;
reverse, inscription: "This [Ephraim] is my son, a favorite to
me." Variant of Jer. 31:20. Ephraim (?–1775), from Berlin,
was court jeweler and mint master to Frederick the Great of
Prussia.

Listed in *Demokritus* by Karl Julius Weber, Vol. VI, Stuttgart, 1843, p. 97

1772   Asher Goldsmid. Same as 1728. "Jew Broker."

David Salomons House, Southborough, Kent, England

ca. 1774   Homage to Moses Mendelssohn. Obverse, bust; reverse, butterfly perched on skull. Medal was issued to honor Mendelssohn, the great German Jewish leader of the Haskalah, for writing *Phaedon*, modeled on the Platonic dialogue. This well-known work was published in 1767.

43 or 44 mm; silver, bronze, and tin; I. Abraham & F. (i.e., Abraham and Son); not dated

Medal is very common and is in many museums and significant private collections.

ca. 1775   Moses Mendelssohn. One-sided medallion with bust and skull.

99 mm; iron; Sahler; not dated

Listed in Moritz Stern's *Aus dem Berliner Jüdischen Museum.* This collection disappeared under the Nazis.

ca. 1780   Mose Benjamin Foà. Obverse, name engraved round printer's mark of Tobias Foà, his ancestor, and palm tree with two lions holding Magen David; reverse is monogram. Mose, born 1729, was court agent to the dukes of Modena and a very prominent Italian book dealer and bibliophile.

30 mm; silver; token

The Jewish Museum, N.Y.C.

ca. 1780   The Wedding of Daniel Abensur and Sara de Castro in Altona (then Danish territory near Hamburg). Obverse, a winged male figure holding a flaming torch upright in one hand and an extinguished torch downward in the other; reverse, inscription referring to the couple and their birth dates in 5513 (i.e., 1753). Nothing more is known of this couple.

35 mm; silver

Danish National Museum, Copenhagen
Listed in Bergsøe's *Dansker Medaljer og Jetons* 1894, No. 1473
Listed in Albert Wolf's *Die Hamburger auf oder von Juden gegprägten Medaillen*

1780   Lord George Gordon. Obverse, bust of Gordon with beard and slouched hat; reverse, inscription "Lord George, Gordon 1780." On rim, "Spence Dealer in Coins London." Lord George Gordon was a prominent English aristocrat and convert to Judaism. The token was issued by Thomas Spence, considered the first English socialist.

English halfpenny size; copper

The Jewish Museum, N.Y.C.
Hebrew Union College Museum, Cincinnati
American Numismatic Society, N.Y.C. (two examples)
Collection of Alfred Rubens, London
Collection of Arthur Polak, Amsterdam
Collection of Abraham E. Millgram, Jerusalem

1793   Lord George Gordon. Obverse, same as above but legend around, "Ld Geo Gordon Died in Newgate Nov 1 1793"; reverses vary. Some rims have above inscription while others are plain.

English halfpenny size; copper

Reverses:
   a. "T. Spence Bookseller Dealer in Prints & Coins," etc.
   b. Britannia seated, and "Rouse Britannia!"
   c. Caduceus and "We were born free and will never die slaves."
   d. Between laurel branches, a hand holding heart and "Honour" above. Below, "James," the name of the engraver.
   e. Cain killing Abel and "Cain" and "Abel" below each figure. "The Begining of Oppression," with the two "n" letters in "Begining" reversed.
   f. Men dancing under a tree and "After the Revolution."
   g. View of building, with "Sessions-House" and "Old Baily."
      Item a—The Jewish Museum, N.Y.C.
      Item b—The Mocatta Library, University College, London; American Numismatic Society, N.Y.C.

Item c—The Jewish Museum, N.Y.C.; Woburn House
Jewish Museum, London

Item d—Hebrew Union College Museum, Cincinnati;
American Numismatic Society, N.Y.C.

Item e—Hebrew Union College Museum, Cincinnati;
Collection of Alfred Rubens, London; American Numismatic Society, N.Y.C.

Item f—Listed by Alfred Rubens in *Anglo-Jewish
Portraits*

Item g—American Numismatic Society, N.Y.C.; Collection of Alfred Rubens, London

1793 Lord George Gordon. Obverse, same as above; reverse, Boys at
Turnstile and "Little Turnstile Halfpenny 1796." This is an example of a mule and the reverse appears on other tokens issued
by Spence.

English halfpenny size; copper

Listed in Dalton and Hamer's *The Provincial Token-Coinage
of the 18th Century* No. 781, p. 171

1790– Daniel Mendoza. All obverses show bust of Mendoza with "D.
1796 Mendoza"; reverses vary. Because of anti-Semitic taunts, the
eighteenth-century English Jews became excellent pugilists and
Mendoza was the most famous English boxing champion of his
age. Issued by T. Spence.

*English halfpenny size; copper (sometimes struck on penny
flan)*

Reverses:
   a. Two pugilists, and "Fashionable Amusement." 1790.
   b. Well-dressed shepherd with crook. 1790.
   c. Boys at turnstile, and "Little Turnstile Halfpenny." This
      is the same reverse that appears on the mule of the Lord
      George Gordon token. 1796.
   d. A youth with a stick, and "A Bridewell Boy." No date.
   e. Breeches burning, and "Pandoras Breeches." No date.
      Item a — Hebrew Union College Museum, Cincinnati;
                American Numismatic Society, N.Y.C.; Col-
                lection of Arthur Polak, Amsterdam; Collec-
                lection of Alfred Rubens, London

Item b — The Jewish Museum, N.Y.C.; Collection of
Alfred Rubens, London; American Numismatic Society, N.Y.C.

Item c — Listed by Alfred Rubens in *Anglo-Jewish
Portraits*

Item d — Woburn House Jewish Museum, London;
Collection of Abraham E. Millgram, Jerusalem

Item e — Collection of Abraham E. Millgram, Jerusalem

1791   Daniel Mendoza, English Jewish boxing champion, with William
Ward, other pugilist. Reverse shows fight between them.

   35 mm; copper and white metal; W. Mainwaring

British Museum, London
Listed by Alfred Rubens in *Anglo-Jewish Portraits*
Listed in Dalton and Hamer's *The Provincial Token-Coinage
of the 18th Century* No. 35, p. 95

1793   Daniel Itzig's Seventieth Birthday. Obverse, bust; reverse, figure
of Charity with child. German banker, director of the Prussian
Mint and patron of the Jewish Free School of Berlin.

   *52 or 53 mm; silver, white metal or tin and copper; Abram-
son*

The Jewish Museum, N.Y.C. (silver and copper)
Hebrew Union College Museum, Cincinnati (silver and copper)
Collection of Alfred Rubens, London (white metal)
Collection of Author, N.Y.C. (silver)
Leo Baeck Institute, N.Y.C. (resilvered)

1794   Homage to Marcus Herz. Obverse, bust; reverse, classical presentation of Pallas, the Greek goddess of wisdom. Herz was a
well-known eighteenth-century German physician and philosopher.

   41 mm; silver and lead; $\frac{A}{S}$ (i.e., Abramson); undated.

The Jewish Museum, N.Y.C. (silver)
National Museum, Jerusalem (silver)

1796   Rachel Lewin. Portrait medallion. Nothing more is known outside
of the sparse description.

   Treck (medalist).

Formerly in Otto Goldschmidt Collection of Gotha, Germany. Medal was not included when the collection was retrieved after World War II.

1797 Moses Lindo, Jr. Same as 1728. "Jew Broker."

Guildhall Museum, London

1803 Seventy-third Birthday of Lippmann Meyer in Breslau. Obverse, bust; reverse, inscription. Issued by "B. F."—Benoni Fried-laender, son of the famous David Friedlaender. Lippmann Meyer was a royal court agent and patron of the Jewish Wilhelm School of Breslau.

38 mm; silver; (Anton Friedrich) Koenig

The Jewish Museum, N.Y.C.
Collection of Bruno Kisch, N.Y.C.

1804 The Wedding of N. W. and L. Kaulla in Stuttgart. Obverse, palm tree surrounded by grapes in a mountainous landscape; reverse, inscription. The Kaullas were a very well-known Jewish family in southwestern Germany.

silver

Listed in Moritz Stern's *Aus dem Berliner Jüdischen Museum.* This collection disappeared under the Nazis.

1809 B. E. Asser in Amsterdam. Commemorating his entry into the Amsterdam Medical Society. Not included in Arthur Polak's book.

Listed in Moritz Stern's *Aus dem Berliner Jüdischen Museum.* This collection disappeared under the Nazis.

1812 Moses da Costa Lindo. Same as 1728. "Jew Broker."

Guildhall Museum, London

5. Medals Commemorating Jewish Activities

1665   Dutch Circumcision Medal. Obverse, anointing of David as king with Hebrew legend indicating a child by the name of David was born on the 5th of Tammuz, 5425 (1665); reverse, King David dancing before the Ark with appropriate Hebrew quotation from 2 Sam. 6:14.

80 mm; gold, with loop; cast and chased

National Museum, Jerusalem
Listed in *Catalogue of Anglo-Jewish Historical Exhibition,* London, 1887, No. 2619

1671   Burial pass permit for Jewish funerals to leave Amsterdam in order to go to the cemeteries outside town. Engraved Jewish star with Hebrew inscriptions on both sides.

42 mm; silver; token

Jewish Historical Museum, Amsterdam

1714   Same as above, except different date.

Jewish Historical Museum, Amsterdam

1747–   Dutch Circumcision Medal. Obverse, date of 5508 in Hebrew
1748   and a pair of scales to signify the just dealings desired for the child in the future; reverse, inscription in Hebrew, "In the city of Dordrecht, Abraham, the son of Hertog [Zangers]."

Listed in H. R. Storer's *Medicina in Nummis* No. 4182

1778   Burial pass permit for the Amsterdam Chevra Kadisha (Burial Society) members to bring corpses to the cemeteries outside town. Obverse, gate with name "Muyderbergh" below and "Let Pass" in Dutch above; reverse, Jewish star engraved in double line and date in Hebrew.

35 mm; silver; perforated in center; token

National Museum, Jerusalem

18th
Century
Same as above. Obverse, gate with name "Isac Burgh" above
and "Let Pass" in Dutch below; reverse, a bier.

39 mm; silver; perforated in center; token; no date

National Museum, Jerusalem

1784
American Circumcision Medal. Obverse, inscription in Hebrew
by mohel recording the circumcision of Moses, son of David
Hays on Monday, 5 Tishri, 5544; reverse, letters "4" and "1" in
Hebrew, possibly standing for "41," the number of children
thus far circumcised by the mohel.

silver; Myers, with trade mark

Listed in *Vol. II of the Lyons Collection*, p. 383, American
Jewish Historical Society, No. 27, 1920

1784
American Circumcision Medal. Similar, except the name indicated
is Israel, son of Isaac Moses.

silver; presumed Myers

Listed in *Vol. II of the Lyons Collection*, p. 383, American
Jewish Historical Society, No. 27, 1920

1788
Talmud Torah, London. Inscription in Hebrew, "Holy Confraternity of Talmud Torah; established A.M. 5492." Probably worn
by the children; institution was predecessor to the Jews' Free
School in London.

brass plaque

Listed in *Great Jewish Portraits in Metal*, D. M. Friedenberg,
ed., p. 20

1791
Jewish Wilhelm School, Breslau, Germany. Obverse, new branch
growing from cut trunk; reverse, inscription.

*21 and 29 mm; silver (listed in Albert Wolf's article,
"Medals," Jewish Encyclopedia, Vol. VIII, 1907, as 11 and
18 mm; but these may be misprints)*

The Jewish Museum, N.Y.C. (29 mm)
Hebrew Union College Museum, Cincinnati (29 mm)
National Museum, Jerusalem (both sizes)

Collection of Abraham E. Millgram, Jerusalem (21 mm)
Collection of Arthur Polak, Amsterdam (29 mm)

1800 Inauguration of the Adat Jeshurun Synagogue (Reform Ashkenazi), Amsterdam. This appears to be the first commemorative medal for a synagogue.

35 mm; bronze engraved

Listed in Polak's *Joodse Penningen in de Nederlanden*. The whereabouts of this medal is unknown.

1808 Prize Medal for Good Conduct of the Brotherhood of Charity and Pity. Italian inscription (city and origin not stated). Obverse, seated allegoric figure and inscription; reverse, inscription. Dated on edge in Hebrew.

44 mm; bronze

The Jewish Museum, N.Y.C.
Woburn House Jewish Museum, London

1810 Building of the Bordeaux Synagogue, France. Inscriptions on both sides. This community, settled by a large group of Marrano refugees, was one of the oldest Jewish groups in France.

35 mm; bronze and pewter; Jaley

The Jewish Museum, N.Y.C. (bronze)
Collection of Arthur Polak, Amsterdam (bronze and pewter)
Collection of the Author, N.Y.C. (bronze)
The Kadman Numismatic Museum, Tel Aviv
Collection of Bruno Kisch, N.Y.C. (bronze)

6. *Miscellanea of Jewish Interest*

1503 Benjamin ben Eliahu Beer. Obverse, classical head, facing right, similar to a Roman emperor, with legends in Hebrew, Latin, and Greek; reverse, Latin legend on raised rim. The date may be read 1497, depending on interpretation. The first and most cryptic of Jewish medals, found near Lyons, France. Apparently cast on order of Benjamin Beer, son of Elijah Beer, a physician.

167 mm; cast bronze; pendent type

Armand II, 142, 16, Anon.

Original in Bibliothèque Nationale de Paris; (probable) copies:
The Jewish Museum, N.Y.C.
Berson Museum, Warsaw
Collection of the late Herman Davidowitz, N.Y.C.
Hebrew Union College Museum, Cincinnati
Lazaro Galdeano Museum, Madrid (lead)
Abraham Wix Religious Museum, Jerusalem (pewter)
The Louvre, Michelangelo Room, Paris
Cluny Museum, Paris (two examples)
Collection of Cecil Roth, Jerusalem
National Museum, Jerusalem (silver; several examples)

1680 German "plague medal." Obverse, view of city of Leipzig; reverse, Aaron with censer among the Jews and comet, moon, and constellations above. "We have seen the staff of God." The frequent diseases sweeping Europe led to the striking of many "plague" or "pestilence" medals. Though the subject matter is Jewish, this may not be a Jewish medal.

39 mm; silver

Listed in Brettauer's *Medicina in Nummis* No. 2270

1696 Joseph de la Penia, shipowner of Holland. Obverse, ships at sea; reverse, inscription in Dutch. Medal given to his ship captain for valorous service in combat with two French men-of-war off Dunkirk.

65 mm; engraved silver (original probably in gold); unique copy

Royal Coin Cabinet, The Hague

1696 Satirical Medal on the Followers of Sabbetai Zevi (1626–76), the Jewish pseudo-Messiah and convert to Islam. Obverse, mountain with lightning and fantastic animals, alchemist and furnace to right; reverse, lamb holding banner on mountain, flying dove with olive branch to left. Latin legends, using the name of Sabbetai as a play on words with biblical quotations referring to the Sabbath from both Old and New Testaments.

44 mm; possibly by Christian Wermuth

Listed in Feill catalog, Frankfurt am Main, 1908, No. 3429

Listed in Robert Ball catalog, *Münze und Medaille*, No. 29,
Sept. 1935, Item No. 37731. Illustrated on Plate I, No. 83

1696   David de Pinto, Holland. Varying inscriptions in Dutch. Six-
stiver piece given to militiamen for protecting his property. A
mob was prevented from sacking de Pinto's house.

28 mm; engraved silver; two specimens known

Jewish Historical Museum, Amsterdam

1768   Hanging of I. Curtis, alias Curtel, for robbery and murder of
Wolf Myers, English Jewish peddler. Dr. Cecil Roth states there
was another medal as well, exhibited in 1944 at the Bodleian
Library, Oxford, from the private collection of Sir Arthur Dixon.

35 mm; copper

Collection of Abraham E. Millgram, Jerusalem

1780   Cabbage Society of London. Obverse, a cabbage or cauliflower;
reverse, the word "Purim," with date.

English halfpenny and farthing sizes; copper or brass

Listed in R. C. Bell's *Tradesmen's Tickets and Private Tokens*
       (1785–1819), p. 44
Listed in Dalton and Hamer's *The Provincial Token-Coinage
       of the 18th Century* No. 1005, p. 191; also No. 1149, p. 205

1786   Presentation of Parnassim of the Portuguese Jews in Amsterdam,
to Petrenella Moens and Adriana van Overstraten. Obverse, peli-
can with young; reverse, engraved inscription in Dutch to persons
receiving award. This was an award for their poem on Esther.

*58 mm; engraved gold; probably two copies; whereabouts
unknown*

Listed in Polak's *Joodse Penningen in de Nederlanden*
Listed in Gerard Van Loon's *Beschrijving van Nederlandische
       Historie-Penningen* (9th vol.), pp. 303 and 304, Amster-
       dam, 1865. Illustrated on Plate LXIV, No. 649

1795   English Private Promissory Token. Obverse, view of Hackney
Church with MCCXC below (1290 being the date of the erection

of the church); reverse, DAR in script capitals with a wreath of laurel above. Issued by David Alves Rebello, a Jewish merchant with a business at London and a private residence at Hackney. Rebello was an enthusiastic coin and art collector. Engraver was John Milton, an assistant medalist at the Royal Mint; later the engraver Jacobs issued a copy with minor variations.

English halfpenny size; 24 impressions in copper and 10 in silver; also penny size in copper; JM (J. Milton)

Woburn House Jewish Museum, London (halfpenny size; copper)
Listed in R. C. Bell's *Tradesmen's Tickets and Private Tokens (1785–1819)*, p. 99
Listed in a variant of 34 mm, copper, in *Médailles et Jetons des Numismates*, by Anthony Durand, p. 167

1796   English Private Commemorative Token. Obverse, same as above but date is to right and name of engraver below; reverse, winged figure of Time before a coin cabinet, holding a tablet inscribed "David Alves Rebello" and legend round, "Memoria in Aeterna." Issued by J. Rebello at the death of David Alves Rebello. There is a later restrike indicating considerable corrosion on the dies.

English penny size; 28 impressions in copper and 8 in silver; J. Milton

Woburn House Jewish Museum, London (copper)
Collection of Alfred Rubens, London (copper)
Listed in R. C. Bell's *Tradesmen's Tickets and Private Tokens (1785–1819)*, p. 101
Listed as 34 mm, silver, in Anthony Durand, *Médailles et Jetons de Numismates*, p. 168

1796   Cabbage Society of London. Same as 1780.

English halfpenny, penny, and twopenny sizes; copper

The Jewish Museum, N.Y.C. (penny size)
Hebrew Union College Museum, Cincinnati (penny size)
Woburn House Jewish Museum, London (penny size)
Collection of Arthur Polak, Amsterdam (penny size)
Collection of Alfred Rubens, London (penny size)

Collection of Author, N.Y.C. (penny size)
American Numismatic Society, N.Y.C. (penny size)
Listed in R. C. Bell's *Tradesmen's Tickets and Private Tokens*
   (1785–1819), p. 43
Listed in Dalton and Hamer's *The Provincial Token-Coinage
   of the 18th Century* (32 mm, Nos. 227 and 227a., p. 118;
   28 mm, No. 1005, p. 544)

1797   English Merchant's Token. Obverse, view of St. Paul's Cathedral;
       reverse, side view of a weaver and legend wishing success to
       manufacturers of Glasgow. On edge, "Payable at M & H Oppen-
       heims Toy Warehouse London."

       English halfpenny size; copper

       Collection of Alfred Rubens, London
       Listed in R. C. Bell's *Commercial Coins (1787–1804)*, p. 115

1799   English Military Award. Obverse, the British lion subduing the
       Indian tiger; reverse, troops moving up for the assault of Seringa-
       patam, Mysore. Awarded for distinguished service at the taking of
       Seringapatam to Samuel Ezekiel Kharcelkar of the Indian Bene
       Israel.

       44 mm; bronze

       Listed as item No. 910 in the *Catalogue of Anglo-Jewish His-
       torical Exhibition, 1887*

1801   Danish Military Award. Obverse, lion with shield on ship bow;
       reverse, crown and crossed swords over laudatory inscription from
       king. Awarded to volunteer Melchior Heymann from Copenhagen,
       for valor in action against the English while manning the blockade
       ship *Jylland*. Name punched on rim.

       54 mm; silver; Gianelli

       Collection of Johan Chr. Holm, Copenhagen

1804   English Private Commemorative Token. Obverse, "Royal Institu-
       tion" above crown from which tree is growing and "1804" below;
       reverse, large "T" and "J A Rebello Esq." Issued after the death
       of J. Rebello (in 1803).

       English halfpenny size; brass

       Hebrew Union College Museum, Cincinnati

Not recorded in R. C. Bell

1804   Hamburg Calendar Medal. Obverse, table showing Sundays of
        year, with Jewish Year 5565 below and a list of the Jewish holi-
        days; reverse, table showing hours when the Free City gates were
        shut.

> *43 mm; gold and silver; Abramson (name of engraver not
> shown)*

Jewish Museum, N.Y.C.
Listed in Gaedechens' *Die neueren Hamburgischen Münzen und
   Medaillen,* Hamburg, 1843, p. 305

1805   Same as above except for change of dates and an added record of
        the dates of the new and full moon during the year.

> *46 mm*

Listed in Gaedechens as above.

1805   Fishmongers Guild of St. Peter's, Amsterdam. Obverse, name of
        society in Dutch; reverse, "ALC" (i.e., Abraham Levi Cohen) and
        "Jood" or Jew, with date. Reverse engraved on blank according to
        name, etc., of member. This was the only guild in which Jews
        could be members.

> *40 mm; copper*

Collection of Arthur Polak, Amsterdam

1814   Cabbage Society of London. Same as 1780. Reverse, however,
        shows crossed branches of palm and laurel with berries. "Purim"
        not shown.

> *English twopenny size; brass*

The Jewish Museum, N.Y.C.
Listed in R. C. Bell's *Tradesmen's Tickets and Private Tokens
   (1785–1819),* p. 239

Collections Reviewed

Amsterdam: Jewish Historical Museum, De Waaghuis
Private Collection of Dr. Arthur Polak

Budapest: The Jewish Museum, Jewish Cultural Center

Cincinnati: Hebrew Union College Museum

Jerusalem: The Bezalel Museum, National Museum
Private Collection of Rabbi Abraham E. Millgram

London: The Jewish Museum, Woburn House
Victoria and Albert Museum
Guildhall Museum
Private Collection of Alfred Rubens
Mocatta Library and Museum, University College

New York: The Jewish Museum
Metropolitan Museum of Art
American Numismatic Society
Private Collection of the late Dr. Bruno Kisch
Private Collection of the Author
Private Collection of the late Herman Davidowitz

Paris: Cabinet des Médailles, Bibliothèque nationale
Museum of Jewish Art

Prague: The Jewish Museum (Medals in the office files)

Tel Aviv: The Kadman Numismatic Museum

Known Jewish Medalists Represented

1. *Anti-Semitic Medals*

None

2. *Marranos and Christian Converts*

None

3. *The Slow Rise of Jewish Emancipation*

1808   Enfranchisement of the Jews of Westphalia—by Abraham Abramson

4. *Medals Commemorating Individual Jews*

1735   Eleazar ben Samuel Shmelka—by Joel, son of Rabbi Lippman Levi

ca. 1774   Homage to Moses Mendelssohn—by Jacob Abraham and his son, Abraham Abramson

1793   Daniel Itzig's Seventieth Birthday—by Abraham Abramson

1794   Homage to Marcus Herz—by Abraham Abramson

5. *Medals Commemorating Jewish Activities*

1784   Circumcision of Moses, son of David Hays—by Myer Myers

1784   Circumcision of Israel, son of Isaac Moses—presumed by Myer Myers

6. *Miscellanea of Jewish Interest*

1804
and
1805   Hamburg Calendar Medals—by Abraham Abramson

7. *Exclusions*

None

Bibliography

1. ALVAREZ-OSSORIO, FRANCISCO. *Catálogo de las Medallas de los Siglos XV y XVI Conservadas en el Museo Arquelógico Nacional*. Madrid, 1950.

2. AMOROS, J. *Medallas de los Acontecimientos Instituciones y Personajes Españoles*. Barcelona, 1958.

3. ARMAND, ALFRED. *Les médailleurs italiens des quinzième et seizième siècles*. 3 vols. Bologna: Arnaldo Forni, 1966.

4. BALL, ROBERT. *Medicina in Nummis*. Berlin, 1950.

5. BELL, R. C. *Commercial Coins (1787–1804)*. Newcastle upon Tyne, England, 1963.

6. BELL, R. C. *Tradesmen's Tickets and Private Tokens (1785–1819)*. Newcastle upon Tyne, England, 1966.

7. BERNHART, MAX. *Archiv für Medaillen-und Plaketten-Kunde Jahrgang III*, No. 3/4/1921–22. Halle: A. D. Saale.

8. BERNHART, MAX. *Medaillen und Plaketten*. 3rd rev. ed. by TYLL KROHA. Braunschweig: Klinkhardt & Biermann, 1966.

9. BINDER, CHRISTIAN. *Württembergische Münz-und Medaillen-Kunde*. Stuttgart, 1846.

10. BLANCHET, ADRIEN. *Manuel de Numismatique française: Tome troisième: Médailles, Jetons, Mereaux*. Paris, 1930.

11. BOLZENTHAL, HEINRICH. *Skizzen zur Kunstgeschichte der modernen Medaillen-Arbeit (1429–1840)*. Berlin, 1840.

12. BRETTAUER, JOSEF. *Medicina in Nummis*. Edited by EDUARD HOLZMAIR. Wien, 1937.

13. CALDECOTT, J. B. *Brokers' Medals and Stockbrokers' Tokens*. Brochure offprint from the Guildhall Library, London. Undated.

14. DALTON, R., and HAMER, S. H. *The Provincial Token-Coinage of the 18th Century*. Middlesex, 1912 and 1913.

15. DOMANIG, KARL. *Die deutsche Medaille in Kunst und Kulturhistorischen Hinsicht*. Wien, 1907

16. DURAND, ANTHONY. *Médailles et Jetons des Numismates*. Geneva, 1865.

17. FEILL, ANTOINE. *Münzen und Medaillen Sammlung* (Auction of Joseph Hamburger). Frankfurt am Main, 1908.

18. FELLNER, EDWARD, and JOSEPH, PAUL. *Die Münzen von Frankfurt am Main*. 4 vols. Frankfurt am Main, 1896.

19. FEUCHTWANGER, H. "Jewish Medals," *Israel Numismatic Bulletin*, No. 5. July, 1963.

20. FIEWEGER, C. *Katalog satyrischer Medaillen und Münzen* (Auction). Berlin, 1885.

20A. FORRER, L. *Biographical Dictionary of Medallists*. 8 vols. London: Spink & Son Ltd., 1904–1912, 1923–1930.

21. FRIEDENBERG, DANIEL M., ed. *Great Jewish Portraits in Medal.* Introduction by Cecil Roth. New York: Schocken Books, 1963.

21A. GORIS, JAN ALBERT. *Étude sur les Colonies marchandes méridionales à Anvers de 1488 à 1567.* Louvain: Librairie Universitaire, 1925.

22. HABICH, GEORG. *Die Deutschen Medailleure des XVI Jahrunderts.* Halle: A. Riechmann & Co., 1916.

22A. HEISS, ALOïSS. *Les Médailleurs de la Renaissance.* 5 vols. Edited by J. Rothschild. Paris, 1892.

23. HERRERA, ADOLFO. *Medallas de Proclamaciones y Juras de los Reyes de España.* Madrid, 1882.

24. HILL, SIR GEORGE F. *The Gustav Dreyfus Collection: Renaissance Medals.* Oxford: Oxford University Press, 1931.

25. HILL, SIR GEORGE F. *The Medallic Portraits of Christ, The False Shekels, The Thirty Pieces of Silver.* Oxford: Clarendon Press, 1920.

26. HOFFMANN, TASSILO. *Jacob Abraham und Abraham Abramson— 55 Jahre Medaillenkunst (1755–1810).* Frankfurt am Main: J. Kauffmann, 1927.

26A. HOFFMEISTER, JACOB. *Hessische Münzen.* Vol. II. Leipzig, 1862.

26B. KIRSCHNER, BRUNO (completed by ARIE KINDLER). *Deutsche Spottmedaillen auf Juden.* Munich: Ernst Battenberg, 1968.

27. KISCH, BRUNO. "Judaica in Nummis." *Historia Judaica,* Vol. VII, 1945.

28. KISCH, GUIDO. "Jewish Personal Medals Without Portraits." *Historia Judaica,* Vol. VII, 1945.

29. LAMAS, JOSE. *Medalhas portuguesas e estrangeiras referentes a Portugal.* Vol. 1. Lisbon, 1916.

30. LÓPES, FERNANDES MANUEL BERNARDO. *Colleccao das medalhas e condecoracoes portuguezas e das estrangeiras con relacao a Portugal.* Lisbon, 1880.

31. MAZEROLLE, FERNAND. *Les Médailleurs français du XVe siècle au milieu du XVIIe siècle.* 3 vols. Paris, 1902–1904.

32. MEISSNER, M. J. "Ueber Christian Wermuth und seine satyrischen Medaillen," in *Blatter für Münzfreunde,* No. 110. July 1, 1883.

33. MERZBACHER, EUGEN. *Münzen und Medaillen aller Länder Munchen* (Auction). 4 March, 1913.

34. NARKISS, M. *Coins of Palestine.* Vol. 1. Jerusalem, 1936.

35. NARKISS, M. "Jewish History in Medals," *B'nai B'rith Magazine.* Vol. XLIV, No. 5, Feb. 1930.

36. PFEIFFER, L. *Pestilentia in Nummis.* Weimar, 1880.

37. PFEIFFER, L., and RULAND, C. *Pestilentia in Nummis.* Tübingen, 1882.

38. PICCIOTTO, JAMES. *Sketches of Anglo-Jewish History.* Republished. London: The Soncino Press, 1956.

39. POLAK, ARTHUR. *Joodse Penningen in de Nederlanden.* Amsterdam: Jacques Schulman, 1958.

40. POLAK, ARTHUR. "Jewish Medals." *Israel Numismatic Journal,* Vol. II, Nos. 1–2, 1964.

41. ROTH, CECIL, ed. *Jewish Art.* New York: McGraw-Hill Book Co., 1961.

42. ROTH, CECIL. *A History of the Marranos.* Philadelphia: The Jewish Publication Society of America, 1932.

43. ROTH, CECIL. *The History of the Jews in Italy.* Philadelphia: The Jewish Publication Society of America, 1946.
44. ROTH, CECIL. *A History of the Jews in England.* Oxford: Oxford University Press, 1941.
45. RUBENS, ALFRED. *Anglo-Jewish Portraits.* London: The Jewish Museum, 1935.
46. RUBENS, ALFRED. *A Jewish Iconography.* London: The Jewish Museum, 1954.
47. STERN, MORITZ. *Die vierte Ausstellung der Kunstsammlung.* Berlin, 1927.
48. STERN, MORITZ. *Aus dem Berliner Jüdischen Museum.* Berlin: Philo, 1937.
49. STORER, HORATIO ROBINSON. *Medicina in Nummis.* Boston, 1931.
50. WOLF, ALBERT. "Medals." *Jewish Encyclopedia,* Vol. VIII, 1907.
51. WOLF, ALBERT. *Die Hamburger auf oder von Juden geprägten Medaillen, Mitteilungen für jüdische Volkskunde,* No. 13, pp. 51–62. Hamburg, 1904.
52. *Historia Hebraica—Ausstellungs—Katalog Jüdische Gemeindehaus.* Berlin, Sept. 1965.
53. *Catalogue of Anglo-Jewish Historical Exhibition.* London: William Clowes and Sons, Ltd., 1887.

Index

Note: Italic page numbers indicate illustrations.